OTHER BOOKS BY BEVERLY A. NEMIRO

with Donna Hamilton
The High Altitude Cookbook
The Complete Book of High Altitude Baking
Colorado a la Carte, Vol. I and II

with Marie von Allman
The Lunch Box Cookbook

THE
Busy People's
COOK BOOK

RANDOM HOUSE

New York

THE *Busy* People's COOKBOOK

Beverly Anderson Nemiro

ISBN: 0–394–46228–9
Library of Congress Catalog Card Number: 79–102308

Manufactured in the United States of America

Book design by Mary M. Ahern

9 8 7 6 5 4 3 2

First Edition

For LENA
who knew the value of time
and who cherished creativity

What are friends, books or health,
the interest of travel, or the delights of home,
if we have not time for their enjoyment?

—*John Lubbock*

Contents

A Grateful Cook

For the most part, I have had the fun (and often quivery feeling) of relying on myself for material in this book. But I could never let it go to press without thanking a magnificent professional, Marjorie Barrett, who gave me guidance, confidence, and encouragement; Gene Koelbel, Peggy Crane, and Gloria Turley, long-time friends, who offered warm understanding, car-pooling, and proofreading help, and always came through with thoughtfully significant suggestions; Robert Trigere, Harold Dillon, Frances Davis, and Ken Pfeiffer, who listened patiently and gave instant help when asked; and my dear husband and children, who were such good sports eating my experiments for eighteen months, and who continuously contributed originality to the recipe invention of the day.

Introduction

This is a cookbook for busy people.

The recipes use many convenience foods—packaged, processed, canned, bottled, refrigerated, dehydrated, and freeze-dried—all those timesaving products festooning the supermarket shelves.

The emphasis is on using those convenience foods in unexpected and unusual ways, *often for a purpose for which they were not intended.*

The recipes are simple, easy to read and follow. The ingredients are available in almost any market. Most of the recipes are short.

There are contemporary, continental, and international dishes for the epicure who is willing to spend a bit more time. There are many for the beginner who wants to cook simply, quickly, and efficiently, and yet with a dash of daring.

These handy new seasonings and packaged foods congenially lend themselves to experimentation, originality, and interesting interpretation.

It is always fun to combine the old with the new. Now, using these inspirative food products, either as a start or as an ingredient, it is possible to make Americanized versions of great classic dishes. All the recipes can easily be prepared by any man, woman, or teen-ager who is willing to use convenience foods in unconventional ways that produce delicious results.

Cooking with convenience foods is not new, as all of us who have ever opened a can of soup know well. But now, the unique and different ways of using them make them practically worth their weight in gold to anyone who has a busy day.

If you possess a spirit of imagination and you wish to serve delectable concoctions that will taste as if you had been in the kitchen for hours, I hope you will venture into this new world of creative cookery, using these delightful timesaving convenience foods, often in ways for which they were *not* intended.

Although the easy recipes in this book have been suggestively placed in Family and Guest sections, there is no substitute for imagination: all can readily be used interchangeably and successfully for family or guest meals. Also, leftover chicken or turkey may be used in recipes calling for frozen chicken.

BEVERLY ANDERSON NEMIRO

Denver, Colorado
March, 1971

Family

A HAPPY FAMILY IS BUT

AN EARLIER HEAVEN.

—*Bowing*

Breakfast

THERE IS NOT A SINGLE MOMENT IN LIFE
THAT WE CAN AFFORD TO LOSE.

—*Goulburn*

Delicious Instant Breakfast

---

1 cup fresh frozen orange juice
1 10-ounce package frozen berries* in instant-thaw pouch
1 egg
½ cup non-fat dry milk powder
1 tablespoon non-dairy creamer powder (optional)
½ cup ice water
Few drops vanilla extract (optional)
1 orange, cut in 6 wedges

ঽ Partially thaw berries, following directions on package. In blender, or mixing bowl, combine all ingredients except orange wedges. Blend at high speed, or beat with mixer, until smooth. Pour into glass mugs or glasses; garnish each with 2 orange wedges. Serve immediately.

3 servings

* Blackberries, strawberries, or red raspberries

Breakfast Pudding

---

1 3¾-ounce package vanilla instant pudding mix
1 17-ounce can fruit cocktail
4 cups cornflakes or crisp rice cereal
½ cup non-dairy whipped topping
1 tablespoon packaged vanilla wafer crumbs

  Have ready 4 to 6 stemmed water goblets, parfait glasses, or mugs (number will be determined by the size you have on hand). Prepare pudding, following directions on package; set aside for 10 to 15 minutes or until almost set. Stir in fruit cocktail and its juice. Spoon into each goblet or glass alternating layers of pudding and cornflakes or rice cereal, ending with pudding. In a separate cup, stir together whipped topping and crumbs. Top each pudding with dollop of mixture.

4 to 6 servings

BAKED EGGS WITH MUSTARD

---

1 4-ounce package (*1 cup*) shredded Cheddar cheese
2 tablespoons butter
¼ cup non-dairy creamer powder
¼ cup water
1 teaspoon prepared mustard
½ teaspoon salt
¼ teaspoon pepper or seasoned pepper
6 eggs, slightly beaten

ৡ➤ Preheat oven to 325° F. Sprinkle cheese in 9-inch square pan or ovenproof dish. Dot with butter. In cup, mix creamer powder, water, mustard, salt, and pepper. Pour half of mixture over cheese. Pour eggs on top, then remaining half of cream mixture. Bake 25 minutes. Serve immediately.

6 servings

Eggs Poached in Chicken Sauce

　1　teaspoon instant minced onion
1½　teaspoons taco seasoning mix or mushroom gravy mix
　　　(*shake package before opening*)
　1　10½-ounce can condensed cream of chicken soup
　¼　teaspoon pepper
　½　cup milk
　6　eggs
　3　English muffins
Paprika or chopped parsley

ટે❧　In medium-sized skillet, stir onion and seasoning or gravy mix into soup. Add pepper and milk. Bring to boil slowly; reduce heat, and add eggs to sauce, one at a time, to poach. Cover. Cook over low heat 15 minutes, or until eggs are set and done to taste. Meanwhile, split, toast, and butter English muffins. Place each half on a plate, top with egg and sauce. Sprinkle with paprika or parsley, or both.

6 servings

Drunken Sausages

---

1 8-ounce package brown-and-serve sausages
½ cup white wine, bourbon, or beef consommé
½ teaspoon instant parsley flakes

ও Prepare sausages, following directions on package, but adding wine, bourbon, or consommé; cover and poach until sausages are done. Serve sprinkled with parsley flakes.   *3 servings*

Chipped Beef on Waffles

---

1 2½-ounce package or jar dried beef
1 cup boiling water
2 3-ounce packages cream cheese with chives, softened
⅓ cup half-and-half cream
1 tablespoon sherry (*optional*)
12 frozen waffles

ও Preheat broiler. Pull or cut beef into small bits*; place in boiling water for 5 minutes; drain. Meanwhile, in small bowl, mash cream cheese with half-and-half and sherry until smooth. Add beef bits. Place waffles on cookie sheet. Spread with beef mixture. Broil slowly, 6 to 8 inches from heat, until heated through and bubbly.
                                                    6 servings

* I use scissors.

French Toast d'Orange

---

4 eggs
½ cup fresh or frozen orange juice
¼ cup orange marmalade
½ teaspoon salt
8 slices firm French or day-old bread
Butter or margarine
Sesame seeds (*optional*)
Powdered sugar

ৡ In shallow dish or pan, beat together eggs, juice, marmalade, and salt. Dip bread slices in mixture, turning to coat each side. Heat about 1 tablespoon butter or margarine at a time in frying pan or on griddle until bubbly. Fry prepared bread, 2 or 3 slices at a time, over medium heat, until light brown on each side, turning only once. Sprinkle top with sesame seeds, if you wish, before turning. Add more butter as you fry additional slices. Serve sprinkled with powdered sugar.

4 to 6 servings

ORANGE SPONGE PANCAKES

---

1 **egg, beaten**
1 **cup half-and-half cream**
¼ **cup frozen orange juice concentrate**
1 **cup packaged pancake mix**
½ **teaspoon instant grated orange peel**

ੴ Preheat pancake griddle, skillet, or electric frying pan. In large mixing bowl, combine egg, cream, and juice concentrate; mix until quite smooth. Stir in pancake mix and orange peel. Batter may be lumpy. Lightly grease griddle. Pour or spoon batter onto hot cooking surface, using tablespoon for silver dollar-size pancakes, and ¼ cup for larger ones. Cook until pancake top is covered with bubbles and edges look cooked. Turn pancake and cook other side. Serve with warm Orange Syrup.

Batter to serve 4 to 6

ORANGE SYRUP

½ **cup frozen orange juice concentrate**
½ **teaspoon instant grated orange peel**
1 **cup sugar**
½ **cup (1 stick) butter**

ੴ Combine all ingredients in medium-sized saucepan. Cook over medium heat until mixture comes to boil, stirring occasionally. Serve warm or at room temperature over pancakes or waffles.

1½ cups

Scottish Waffles

1½ cups packaged pancake mix
 2 tablespoons sugar
 ½ cup quick-cooking rolled oats
 ¼ teaspoon cinnamon
 3 tablespoons currants, raisins, or chopped nuts
 2 eggs, beaten
1½ cups milk
 ⅓ cup melted butter

༄ Preheat waffle iron. In large mixing bowl, combine and mix together pancake mix, sugar, oats, cinnamon, and currants, raisins, or nuts. In medium-sized bowl, combine eggs and milk; stir into dry ingredients. Stir in butter. Pour or spoon batter into heated waffle iron, filling baker ⅔ full. Stir batter before each pouring to keep it blended. Bake until golden brown, and steaming stops. These waffles are good with Honey and Orange Spread, opposite.

Batter to serve 4

Honey and Orange Spread

---

1 **cup** (*2 sticks*) **butter, softened**
⅓ **cup honey**
1 **to 2 teaspoons instant grated orange peel**
2 **tablespoons frozen orange juice concentrate**

&ewline; In small mixing bowl, cream butter with honey until light and fluffy. Add orange peel and juice concentrate; beat until blended. Cover; store in refrigerator. For easy spreading, allow to stand at room temperature for 30 minutes before serving.

1½ cups

Gingerbread Waffles

½ cup (*1 stick*) melted butter or margarine
¼ cup *warm* water
1 14½-ounce package gingerbread mix
2 egg yolks, beaten
2 egg whites, beaten until soft peaks form

ౘ Preheat waffle iron. In large mixing bowl, blend together butter and warm water. Add gingerbread mix. Beat 2 minutes at medium speed on mixer, or vigorously by hand. Stir in egg yolks. Gently fold in egg whites. Pour or spoon batter into heated waffle iron, filling baker ⅔ full. Bake until steaming stops. Serve immediately with Whipped Ginger Topping, or warmed applesauce, or both.

Batter to serve 4 to 6

Whipped Ginger Topping

---

1 cup non-dairy whipped topping
⅛ teaspoon nutmeg
Slivered crystallized ginger

ౘ In small bowl, fold into topping nutmeg and slivered ginger to taste. Serve chilled.   *1 cup*

Upside-down Sausage Cake

1⅓ cups packaged biscuit mix
 ¾ cup sugar
 3 tablespoons buttery-type salad oil
 1 egg, slightly beaten
 ¾ cup buttermilk
 1 teaspoon vanilla extract
 ¼ teaspoon nutmeg
 ¼ teaspoon cinnamon
12 brown-and-serve sausages

୧ଛ Preheat oven to 350° F. Butter or grease 8-inch square baking dish. In large mixing bowl, combine all ingredients except sausages; beat until well blended. Arrange sausages in bottom of prepared dish. Pour or spoon batter over sausages. Bake 30 to 40 minutes, or until top of cake springs back when touched lightly with fingertips. Remove from oven; cool 5 minutes; invert on serving platter. Serve warm.

6 servings

DATE RING

¼ cup (½ *stick*) melted butter
1 8- or 10-ounce package chopped pitted dates
½ cup brown sugar, firmly packed
1 teaspoon cinnamon
½ cup chopped nuts
1 8-ounce package refrigerated biscuits

৯ Preheat oven to 425° F. Brush bottom of 8-inch layer cake pan with half the melted butter. Arrange dates in pan, leaving a 3-inch circle vacant in center. With fork, fluff up sugar and sprinkle over dates; then sprinkle with cinnamon and nuts. With sharp knife, cut biscuits in fourths. Arrange evenly over dates, sides touching, leaving circle open in center of pan. Brush with remaining butter. Bake 10 minutes, or until done. Do not overbake. To serve, cool, invert on plate, then pull apart or use sharp knife to cut into pieces.

About 6 servings

Applesauce Muffins

---

2 cups packaged biscuit mix
¼ cup sugar
¾ teaspoon cinnamon
⅛ teaspoon nutmeg
½ cup applesauce
¼ cup milk
1 egg, slightly beaten
2 tablespoons cooking oil

ᔐ Preheat oven to 400° F. Grease 2-inch muffin pan cups. In medium-sized mixing bowl, combine biscuit mix, sugar, cinnamon, and nutmeg. In small bowl, combine applesauce, milk, egg, and oil. Add to dry ingredients, mixing vigorously until well blended. Fill muffin pan cups ⅔ full. Bake 12 minutes, or until golden and done.

12 muffins

Pineapple Pecan Muffins

---

1 14-ounce package orange muffin mix
1 8¾-ounce can crushed pineapple, drained (*reserve syrup*)
⅔ cup half-and-half cream
¼ teaspoon instant grated orange peel
1 egg, beaten
¼ cup (½ *stick*) melted butter or margarine
⅓ cup chopped pecans
1 3-ounce package cream cheese, softened

ৡ Preheat oven to 400° F. Grease 2½-inch muffin pan cups. In medium-sized mixing bowl, combine muffin mix, pineapple, cream, orange peel, and egg. Stir to moisten all ingredients, but do not overbeat. Fill muffin pan cups ⅔ full. Bake 15 to 20 minutes, or until golden brown and done. Remove each muffin from pan. Dip warm muffin tops in melted butter, then in pecans; set aside. In small bowl, mash together cream cheese and 2 to 3 teaspoons reserved pineapple syrup. Use as spread for warm muffins.

9 muffins

Lunch

KNOW THE VALUE OF TIME;

SNATCH, SEIZE, AND ENJOY EVERY MOMENT

OF IT.

—Lord Chesterfield

PEASANT SOUP

2½ cups water
1 tablespoon instant celery flakes
1 teaspoon instant minced onion
1 cup cream
1 teaspoon salt
¼ teaspoon white pepper
3 tablespoons butter
⅔ cup instant mashed potato flakes
3 to 4 tablespoons frozen leaf spinach
Croutons or popped popcorn

ટુ❧ Heat water to boiling in medium-sized saucepan. Stir in celery flakes and onion. Reduce heat; simmer 3 minutes. Add cream, salt, pepper, butter, and potato flakes; stir with long-tined fork. Simmer 2 minutes. Remove spinach from package. With very sharp knife, cut off the 4 corners and add them to soup. They will defrost instantly. (Return unused frozen spinach to package, seal, and return it to freezer for future use.) Stir soup until spinach wilts into it. Serve hot, but not boiling, with crouton or popcorn garnish.

6 servings

New England Clam Chowder

2 10¼-ounce cans frozen cream of potato soup
2 soup cans milk
2 7½-ounce cans minced clams, undrained
2 tablespoons butter
Thinly sliced green onions
Ground mace (*optional*)

ᔰ In heavy saucepan, combine soup, milk, clams with juice, and butter. Cover. Heat through, but do not boil. Serve garnished with onion slices and breath of mace.

6 servings

Pizza Soup

2 10¾-ounce cans condensed tomato soup
2 soup cans water
3 teaspoons taco seasoning mix (*shake package before opening*)
1 4-ounce package (*1 cup*) shredded mozzarella cheese
1 cup packaged croutons

ᔰ In large saucepan, combine and heat soup, water, and seasoning mix, stirring with wire whisk or slotted spoon to blend completely. When soup comes to boil, stir in cheese. Remove from heat immediately, so cheese does not melt. Serve topped with croutons.   *6 servings*

Chicken Chop Suey

1½ cups diced celery
1 medium onion, thinly sliced
2 tablespoons cooking oil
1 10½-ounce can chicken consommé
2 tablespoons cornstarch
1 medium green pepper, cut into very thin strips
2 tablespoons soy sauce
2 tablespoons molasses
1 1-pound can bean sprouts, rinsed and drained
1 5-ounce can water chestnuts, drained and sliced
1 7-ounce package (*2 cups*) frozen cooked and diced chicken
1 5-ounce can bamboo shoots

≳ In large skillet, sauté celery and onion in hot oil until onion is transparent but not browned (about 3 minutes). Add 1 cup of the consommé; stir cornstarch into remaining consommé, then stir into onion mixture. Add remaining ingredients; cook over medium heat until liquid is just thickened. Serve with rice.

4 to 5 servings

CONTENTED CHICKEN CASSEROLE

---

2 cups instant mashed potato flakes
2 tablespoons butter or margarine
1 small onion, chopped
1 tablespoon instant parsley flakes
1½ 7-ounce packages (*3 cups*) frozen cooked and diced
    chicken
1 tablespoon bottled aromatic bitters
1 8-ounce can tomato sauce
⅓ cup ketchup
1 6-ounce can mushrooms and juice
4 hard-cooked eggs, peeled and sliced
½ cup sliced almonds
1 4-ounce package (*1 cup*) shredded Cheddar cheese

꿈 Prepare potatoes, following directions on package. Preheat oven to 450° F. Melt butter in skillet, over medium heat; sauté onion and parsley flakes until onion is limp. Add chicken, bitters, tomato sauce, ketchup, and mushrooms with juice. Bring just to boil, reduce heat, and simmer 5 minutes. Generously butter 2-quart oven-proof casserole. Spoon potatoes on bottom of casserole; top with chicken mixture. Arrange egg slices over chicken; sprinkle with almonds and cheese. Bake 20 minutes, or until cheese is melted and casserole is well heated through.   *6 to 8 servings*

BROILED CHICKEN CALYPSO

---

1 2- to 2½-pound broiler-fryer chicken, cut into fourths
1 envelope onion soup mix
1 6-ounce can frozen orange juice concentrate, thawed
¾ cup water
1 unpeeled orange, cut into 8 slices

ঽ• Preheat broiler. Wash and pat dry chicken pieces. Place them, skin side down, in bottom of broiler pan (use no rack). In bowl, combine soup mix, juice concentrate, and water; mix well. Brush chicken with mixture. Broil 5 to 7 inches from heat for 20 minutes, or until lightly browned, brushing occasionally with sauce. Turn; broil 15 to 20 minutes more. When drumstick moves easily, chicken is done. Serve garnished with orange slices. (This can be cooked over glowing charcoal, too.)

4 servings

ESCALLOPED CHICKEN

---

4 cups cheese-flavored puffs
4 hard-cooked eggs, peeled and sliced
1½ 7-ounce packages (*3 cups*) frozen cooked and diced
    chicken
¾ cup chopped celery
1 10½-ounce can condensed cream of chicken or celery
    soup
1 10½-ounce can condensed cream of mushroom soup
⅔ cup white wine, chicken broth, or water

ৡ Preheat oven to 350° F. Generously butter bottom and sides of 2½-quart casserole. Cover bottom with 2 cups cheese puffs. Arrange egg slices, chicken, and celery on top of puffs. In bowl, combine and mix soups and wine, broth, or water. Pour over eggs and chicken. Cover with remaining 2 cups cheese puffs. Bake 45 minutes to 1 hour, or until chicken is cooked through and casserole is bubbly. Serve with Pimiento Sauce, below, if you enjoy a rich topping to an already rich dish.

6 servings

PIMIENTO SAUCE

---

1 10¾-ounce can condensed Cheddar cheese soup
½ cup milk
2 tablespoons chopped pimiento
1 to 2 tablespoons white wine (*optional*)

ৡ Combine all ingredients in saucepan. Cook and stir over medium heat until well heated through. Serve hot. This sauce is excellent served with veal, fish, vegetables, and omelets.

1½ cups

TUNA SALAD WITH AVOCADO DRESSING

---

1 small head iceberg lettuce, torn into bite-size pieces
2 tomatoes, peeled and chopped
1 4½-ounce can (½ *cup*) chopped ripe olives
1 cup corn chips
1 7-ounce can albacore tuna fish, drained and flaked
1 7¾-ounce can frozen avocado dip, thawed
½ cup cream-style cottage cheese
¼ cup grated Parmesan cheese
¼ cup salad oil

ૐ In salad bowl, combine lettuce, tomatoes, olives, corn chips, and tuna fish; toss lightly. In separate small bowl, combine and beat avocado dip, cottage cheese, Parmesan cheese, and salad oil. Pour over salad; toss lightly but well.

6 servings

TUNA FISH AND ASPARAGUS PARMIGIANA

---

2 10-ounce packages frozen asparagus cuts
1 10½-ounce can (*1¼ cups*) white sauce
2 6½-ounce cans tuna fish, drained and flaked
2 tablespoons wine or cream
¼ teaspoon ground coriander
½ cup grated Parmesan cheese
½ cup crushed potato chips
Paprika

ટે Preheat oven to 350° F. Very generously butter 10 × 6 × 2-inch baking dish. In saucepan, cook asparagus following directions on package, but cook for half the time directed. Arrange half-cooked asparagus in prepared dish. In bowl, combine white sauce, tuna fish, wine or cream, and coriander, mixing to blend very well. Sprinkle cheese over asparagus. Pour cream and tuna sauce over cheese. Sprinkle with potato chips and paprika. Bake 30 minutes.

4 to 6 servings

Tuna Custard

½ 8-ounce package (*1¾ cups*) herb-seasoned stuffing mix
2 7-ounce cans albacore tuna fish, drained and flaked
4 tablespoons butter or margarine
¼ cup flour
⅛ teaspoon salt
Freshly ground pepper
2 cups chicken broth
3 eggs, slightly beaten

8→ Preheat oven to 325° F. In bowl, prepare stuffing mix, following directions on package for dry stuffing. Spread in 10 × 6 × 1½-inch baking dish. Arrange tuna fish over stuffing. In saucepan, melt butter or margarine; blend in flour, salt, and pepper to taste. Add broth. Cook and stir over medium heat until mixture is smooth and thickened. Stir a bit of hot mixture into beaten eggs, then stir eggs into hot sauce. Pour over tuna fish. Bake 35 minutes, or until a knife inserted in center of custard comes out clean. Let stand 5 minutes, then cut into squares to serve. This is delicious served with Pimiento Sauce, page 26.

6 servings

CASSEROLE VERACRUZANA

---

2 teaspoons instant minced onion
2 1-pound cans stewed tomatoes
2 eggs, beaten
½ cup milk
2 teaspoons chili powder
1 teaspoon salt
¼ teaspoon cumin (*comino*) powder
1 tablespoon instant parsley flakes
3 6½-ounce cans tuna fish, drained and flaked
1 5-ounce package tortilla chips
1 4-ounce package (*1 cup*) shredded Cheddar cheese
2 cups shredded Monterey Jack cheese
1 cup commercial sour cream

ʒ✺ Preheat oven to 325° F. Stir 1 teaspoon onion into each can of tomatoes; set aside. In large bowl, combine eggs, milk, chili powder, salt, cumin, and parsley flakes; beat with wire whisk to blend. Add tomatoes and tuna fish; mix well. Place half the tortilla chips on bottom of 3-quart ovenproof casserole. Spoon half the tuna mixture over chips; cover with half of the cheeses and half of the sour cream. Repeat process: layer of chips, tuna, cheeses, and sour cream. Bake 40 minutes, or until well heated through and bubbly.   *8 servings*

STUFFED PEPPER CUPS IN SPAGHETTI SAUCE

---

6 medium green peppers
2 15½-ounce cans corned beef hash
1 4-ounce package (*1 cup*) shredded Cheddar cheese
¼ teaspoon pepper or seasoned pepper
1 teaspoon instant parsley flakes
½ teaspoon crumbled sweet basil
1 2¼-ounce package dry spaghetti sauce mix

ৡ∾ Preheat oven to 375° F. Wash green peppers, cut away stem ends, remove seeds, and cut off thin slice from bottom of each so peppers will stand level. In large pan of boiling water, boil peppers 4 to 5 minutes, uncovered; drain. Meanwhile, in large bowl, combine hash, half the cheese, pepper, parsley flakes, and sweet basil. Toss lightly but well to mix thoroughly. Stuff peppers with this mixture. Make spaghetti sauce, following directions on package. Pour sauce in flat 2-quart baking dish; arrange stuffed peppers in sauce. Bake 30 minutes. Remove from oven; sprinkle with remaining ½ cup cheese. Bake 10 minutes more, or until cheese is melted and bubbly. Serve in dish peppers were baked in, spooning sauce over top of peppers as they are served.

6 servings

CORNISH STYLE PASTIES

½ pound ground beef
1 tablespoon chopped onion
1 teaspoon taco, chili, or sloppy joe seasoning mix (*shake package before opening*)
½ teaspoon salt or seasoning salt
⅛ teaspoon freshly ground pepper
1 8-ounce package refrigerated biscuits (*10 biscuits*)
1 4-ounce package (*1 cup*) shredded Cheddar or other cheese

ʒ❧ Preheat oven to 425° F. In skillet, over medium heat, combine beef, onion, seasoning mix, salt, and pepper. Cook until meat is browned, chopping it into small granules as it cooks. To make each pasty, use 2 whole biscuits. Roll each biscuit out to 5-inch long oval on well-floured board. On each of 5 ovals place 3 tablespoons meat mixture and sprinkle with cheese. Cover with remaining 5 ovals, moistening edges with water and tightly sealing with tines of fork. Prick top of pasty with fork, or cut slits, to allow steam to escape during cooking. Bake 8 to 10 minutes, or until golden. Serve hot as a sandwich, or place on lunch or dinner plate, topped with steak sauce, ketchup, mustard, or a combination of these.   5 *servings*

HAMBURGER PATTIES A LA PARMESAN

1½ pounds ground beef
⅔ cup packaged biscuit mix
⅓ cup tomato juice
 1 egg, slightly beaten, or ¼ cup red wine
 2 teaspoons instant sweet pepper flakes
½ teaspoon dried dill weed
 1 small clove garlic, minced
Dash of nutmeg
¾ teaspoon salt
Parmesan cheese

৯৯   Preheat oven to 400° F. Grease flat 2-quart baking dish. In mixing bowl, combine and mix all ingredients, except cheese. Toss lightly to mix. Let stand 10 minutes. Shape into 6 patties, round more than flat in shape. Place in prepared dish. Bake 20 minutes, for medium, or longer to taste. Remove from oven; sprinkle each patty with cheese, and return to oven for 2 minutes. Serve on bed of generously buttered noodles.

6 servings

HAMBURGERS MEXICANA

1½ pounds ground beef
1 tablespoon freeze-dried chopped chives
1 envelope chili seasoning mix
6 hamburger buns (*optional*)
1 ripe avocado, peeled and cut into 12 slices
Commercial sour cream

ह‍ॐ In medium-sized bowl, combine beef, chives, and chili mix; toss lightly but well. Shape into 6 patties. Pan-fry, broil, or cook over glowing charcoal until done as desired. Serve patties in hamburger buns, sandwich style, or on luncheon or dinner plate, topping each with two slices of avocado and dollop of sour cream.

6 servings

Open-face Hamburgers Jamaican

---

3 hamburger buns, cut in half
2 pounds ground beef
1 to 2 teaspoons packaged bacon salad dressing mix
  (*shake package before opening*)
2 tablespoons water, consommé, or wine
1 large onion, cut into 6 slices
2 tablespoons butter or margarine
2 tablespoons bottled thick steak sauce
1 13½-ounce can crushed pineapple, drained
1 large tomato, cut into 6 slices

ᔭ Toast hamburger bun halves; set aside. In mixing bowl, combine beef, salad dressing mix, and water, consommé, or wine; toss lightly but well. Shape into 6 patties. Pan-fry or broil patties until done as desired (about 4 to 5 minutes, or longer, on each side). While patties cook, in skillet, sauté onion slices in butter or margarine, until cooked and soft or golden, turning once. On each toasted bun half, place slice of sautéed onion, meat patty, teaspoon steak sauce, 1 tablespoon or more pineapple, and slice of tomato. Broil until warmed through. Serve open-face style immediately.

6 servings

HOEDOWN HAMBURGERS

---

2 pounds ground beef
1 envelope onion soup mix
½ cup tomato juice
1 1-pound can pork and beans
2 tablespoons sweet pickle relish
¼ cup ketchup
3 tablespoons prepared mustard
1 teaspoon Worcestershire sauce
2 tablespoons instant celery flakes
½ teaspoon salt or seasoning salt
8 hamburger buns, cut in half

&~ In medium-sized bowl, combine beef, soup mix, and juice; toss lightly to mix. Shape into 8 patties. Broil, pan-fry, or cook over glowing charcoal until done as desired. Meanwhile, in medium-sized saucepan, partially mash pork and beans with tines of fork or back of spoon. Add relish, ketchup, mustard, Worcestershire sauce, celery flakes, and salt. Heat, stirring to blend flavors. Place buns, opened, on serving plates or large platter. Place cooked hamburger patty on each bun bottom, cover with bean sauce and top of bun.

8 servings

POTATO-HAMBURGER PANCAKE

---

1 package (*4 servings*) instant potato pancake mix
1 pound lean ground beef
½ cup diced green pepper
1 teaspoon instant minced onion
1 tablespoon instant celery flakes
1 tablespoon salad or cooking oil
1 teaspoon salt or seasoning salt
½ teaspoon pepper
1 teaspoon crumbled sweet basil
1 8-ounce can tomato sauce

৪৯ In bowl, prepare pancake batter, following directions on package; let stand 10 minutes. Meanwhile, in
skillet, sauté beef, green pepper, onion, and celery flakes
in oil, chopping meat into small granules as it cooks.
Preheat broiler. Drain any excess fat from meat. Stir salt,
pepper, sweet basil, and tomato sauce into beef. Spread
potato pancake batter over beef in skillet, as in frosting a
cake. Continue cooking 5 minutes. Place under preheated
broiler 5 minutes. Serve immediately.

4 to 5 servings

GROUND BEEF NUGGETS

1½ pounds ground beef
½ pound ground pork
1 3¾-ounce package 4-minute meat loaf mix
2 eggs, slightly beaten
⅔ cup red wine or cold water
Bottled beef gravy and seasoning base

ॐ Preheat oven to 400° F. In bowl, combine beef, pork, meat loaf mix, eggs, and wine or water. Toss lightly to mix. Shape into 6 large or 12 small round balls. Place in shallow baking pan. Brush tops with liquid gravy base. Bake 20 minutes for small nuggets; 30 minutes for large nuggets; or until done to taste.   *6 servings*

AZTEC CHILI

1½ pounds ground beef
2 tablespoons cooking oil
1 envelope (*1¾ ounces*) chili seasoning mix
1 1-pound can peeled tomatoes
1 1-pound can kidney beans
½ cup tomato juice or water
Dash of garlic salt
¼ teaspoon cumin (*comino*) powder

ॐ In skillet, brown beef in hot oil, chopping it into small granules as it cooks. Drain off excess fat. Sprinkle seasoning mix over meat; stir well. Add remaining ingredients; bring to boil, stirring to blend flavors. Reduce heat; cover, and simmer 15 minutes.   *6 servings*

Stroganoff Casserole

1 5½-ounce package instant mashed potatoes
1 1⅜-ounce package sour cream sauce mix
⅔ cup milk
1 10½-ounce can (*1¼ cups*) white sauce
2 cups diced leftover beef or 1 pound frankfurters, cut
    into chunks
1 3½-ounce can French fried onion rings
1 teaspoon salt or seasoning salt
Lemon pepper
¼ cup grated Parmesan cheese

ॐ Preheat oven to 350° F. Butter 13 × 8¾ × 2-inch baking dish. Prepare potatoes, following directions on package. Spread in prepared dish. In bowl, combine sour cream sauce mix, milk, white sauce, beef or frankfurters, onion rings, and salt; let stand 5 minutes. Spoon over potatoes. Sprinkle with pepper to taste and cheese. Bake 30 minutes.

6 servings

ENCHILADAS EL MOLINO

---

10 frankfurters
10 refrigerated, canned, or frozen and thawed corn tor-
    tillas*
1½ 4-ounce packages (1½ cups) shredded Cheddar cheese
1 10-ounce can enchilada sauce

ও◈ Preheat oven to 400° F. Wrap each frankfurter in a
tortilla; skewer closed with toothpick. Place in shallow
baking dish. Sprinkle with cheese. Pour enchilada sauce
over cheese. Bake 12 minutes, or until cheese is bubbly
and frankfurters are heated through.   5 servings

* Tortillas dry out unless baked immediately.

TAOS TAMALE PIE

---

1 pound ground beef
1 envelope taco seasoning mix
1 1-pound can tomatoes, cut up (with juice)
1 12-ounce can whole kernel corn, drained
1 4½-ounce can (½ cup) chopped ripe olives
1 7- to 10-ounce package corn muffin or corn bread mix
1 teaspoon caraway seed and/or instant sweet pepper
    flakes

ও◈ Preheat oven to 400° F. In medium-sized skillet,
over high heat, quickly brown beef, chopping it into small

granules as it cooks. Stir in seasoning mix, tomatoes, corn, and olives. Heat mixture through, stirring to blend ingredients. Meanwhile, prepare corn muffin or corn bread mix, following directions on package, but adding caraway seed and/or pepper flakes. Spoon meat mixture into shallow 2-quart casserole or baking dish; spoon corn muffin mixture over top. Bake 15 to 20 minutes, or until top is golden brown and done.   *5 to 6 servings*

Louisiana Casserole
(*Sweet Potato-Canadian Bacon Casserole*)

---

1 5-ounce package instant yams (*Louisiana sweet potatoes*)
1 egg, beaten
2 tablespoons brown sugar, firmly packed
¼ teaspoon salt
¼ cup chopped or broken walnuts or pecans
1 13½-ounce can crushed pineapple and juice
8 slices (*1 pound*) Canadian-style bacon
8 walnut halves

ह्ल Preheat oven to 350° F. Butter 1-quart casserole. Prepare yams, following directions on package. Cool. Fold in egg, sugar, salt, nuts and 3 tablespoons pineapple with juice. Spoon into prepared casserole. Arrange bacon slices on top, and put spoonful of pineapple and 1 walnut half on each bacon slice. Bake 30 minutes.

4 servings

HAM JEWEL CASSEROLE

---

1 9-ounce package frozen Italian beans
1 9-ounce package frozen cut wax beans
6 4 X 4 X ⅛-inch slices (*about 1 pound*) cooked ham
1 10¾-ounce can condensed Cheddar cheese soup
1 15½-ounce can sliced pineapple, drained (*reserve juice*)
½ cup commercial sour cream
1 2-ounce jar sliced pimientos, drained

ᔿ Cook both packages of beans, following directions on package; drain. Butter large flat baking dish; arrange beans on bottom of dish. Place ham slices over beans. In bowl, combine soup, reserved pineapple juice and sour cream; beat with wire whisk or spoon until smooth. Pour or spoon over ham. Arrange pineapple slices on top of sauce. Decorate with pimiento slices. Bake at 325° F. for 45 minutes.

6 servings

Hot Potato Salad Bavarian

---

1 12-ounce package frozen hash brown potatoes
1 1-pound can peas, drained
1 2-ounce jar sliced pimiento, drained
1 cup mayonnaise
½ cup bottled French dressing
½ cup commercial sour cream
2 tablespoons instant parsley flakes
1 teaspoon salt or seasoning salt
Paprika

ટ‌જ Preheat oven to 350° F. Prepare potatoes, following directions on package. Grease 1½- to 2-quart baking dish or casserole. In large bowl, or in pan potatoes were cooked in, combine potatoes and remaining ingredients, except paprika, mixing lightly. Spoon into prepared baking dish. Sprinkle with paprika. Bake 20 minutes. Serve hot.

6 servings

Concord Grape Mold

2 cups grape juice
1 3-ounce package Concord grape gelatin
1 tablespoon packaged cornflake or vanilla wafer crumbs
1 teaspoon sugar
1 cup yogurt or whipped cream

᠒᠍᠍᠍ In saucepan, heat grape juice just to boiling. Dissolve gelatin in it. Pour into 2-cup mold or 4 individual custard cups or molds. Chill until firm. Mix together crumbs and sugar. Unmold gelatin onto serving plate or plates. Serve topped with generous dollop of yogurt or whipped cream, and sprinkle with sweetened crumbs.

4 servings

Bean, Corn, and Olive Salad

---

1 envelope sloppy joe seasoning mix
½ cup water
¼ cup wine vinegar
¼ cup salad oil
1 12-ounce can whole kernel corn, drained
1 1-pound can cut green beans
1 cup pitted ripe olives
¼ cup sliced green onions and tops
1 tablespoon chopped pimiento

ঽ In small bowl, combine seasoning mix with water, vinegar, and salad oil; blend with fork; set aside. In salad bowl, combine remaining ingredients; toss lightly. Add dressing; toss lightly but well. Serve chilled.

6 to 7 servings

Oven Shy Brownies

---

3 cups packaged vanilla wafer crumbs
2 cups miniature marshmallows
¾ cup chopped pecans
1 cup powdered sugar, sifted
1 12-ounce package (2 *cups*) semi-sweet chocolate bits
1 cup evaporated milk
⅛ teaspoon cinnamon
Few grains nutmeg

&~ Butter 9-inch square pan. In large mixing bowl, combine crumbs, marshmallows, pecans and sugar; mix very well. In medium-sized saucepan, combine chocolate bits, milk, cinnamon, and nutmeg. Heat over low heat until chocolate bits are melted, stirring with wire whisk to make smooth. Set aside ½ cup chocolate mixture for glaze; add remaining chocolate to crumb mixture; mix very well. Spread in prepared pan. Spread with reserved glaze. Chill. Cut into squares.

36 squares

Rocky Roads

---

1 1-pound 6½-ounce package fudge brownie mix
2 tablespoons butter
½ cup semi-sweet chocolate bits
3 tablespoons hot water
1 cup powdered sugar
½ cup chopped walnuts
2 cups miniature marshmallows

ॐ Make and bake brownies, following directions on package. Meanwhile, melt butter in medium-sized saucepan, over low heat. Stir in chocolate bits and hot water; blend well. Remove from heat. Stir in sugar and walnuts. Sprinkle baked hot brownies with marshmallows when they are removed from oven. Pour chocolate sauce over marshmallows. Cool. Cut into squares.

About 4 dozen squares

Turtles

1 1-pound 1½-ounce package fudge cake mix
½ cup peanut, corn, or vegetable oil
2 tablespoons water
2 eggs
1 8-ounce package large pecan halves

ᖰᴥ Preheat oven to 375° F. Generously butter cookie sheets. In medium-sized mixing bowl, combine all ingredients, except pecans; mix thoroughly, set aside. Arrange clusters of three pecan halves on buttered sheets. Roll dough into 1-inch balls. Cover each pecan cluster with dough ball; flatten slightly with tines of fork or back of spoon. Bake 8 to 10 minutes, or until done. Cool, then spread with canned frosting or Chocolate Frosting, below.

4 to 5 dozen

Chocolate Frosting

1 tablespoon peanut, corn, or vegetable oil
2 tablespoons cocoa powder
½ teaspoon vanilla extract
1 cup powdered sugar, sifted
2 tablespoons cream

ᖰᴥ In small bowl, mix oil and cocoa; add vanilla. Stir in sugar and cream. Add more powdered sugar if frosting is too thin, more cream if too thick. Use frosting immediately for proper spreading consistency.

SCOTCH CRUNCHIES

½ cup smooth-style peanut butter
1 6-ounce package (*1 cup*) butterscotch bits
2½ cups pre-sweetened cornflakes
½ cup nuts

ह‍ In top of double boiler, over simmering water, combine and melt peanut butter and butterscotch bits; stir to make smooth. When completely blended, remove from heat; stir in cereal flakes and nuts. Drop by teaspoonfuls onto waxed paper. Refrigerate until firm.

About 2 dozen

CRISPY CHEWS

---

16 (*4½ ounces*) vanilla caramels
¼ cup semi-sweet chocolate bits
¼ cup miniature marshmallows
2 cups crisp rice cereal or canned chow mein noodles

ह‍ In medium-sized saucepan, over medium-low heat, melt caramels, chocolate bits, and marshmallows in 1 tablespoon water; stir until mixture is well combined and blended. Pour over cereal; stir and toss until cereal is coated with mixture. Drop by teaspoonfuls onto waxed paper. Allow to set until firm.   *About 2 dozen*

German Chocolate Cookies

---

1 1-pound 2½-ounce package German chocolate flavor
   cake mix
½ cup peanut, corn, or vegetable oil
¼ cup water
1 egg
1 3½-ounce can or 1 4-ounce package flaked coconut

 Preheat oven to 375° F. In medium-sized mixing
bowl, combine cake mix, oil, water, and egg; mix
thoroughly. Stir in coconut. Drop by teaspoonfuls onto
ungreased cookie sheet. Bake about 12 minutes, or until
done. Cool on cookie sheet 1 minute, then remove immediately to wire rack or paper toweling, or cookies will
stick.

4½ dozen

Chocolate Peanut Butter Drops

---

2 cups sugar
½ cup (*1 stick*) butter or margarine
½ cup milk
¼ cup cocoa
2 tablespoons non-dairy creamer powder
¼ teaspoon salt
½ cup peanut butter
3½ cups quick-cooking rolled oats
1 teaspoon vanilla extract

෧෨ In large saucepan, combine sugar, butter, milk, cocoa, creamer powder, and salt. Stir, cooking over medium heat, until mixture comes to a full boil. Remove from heat. Stir in peanut butter, rolled oats, and vanilla; mix thoroughly. Drop by teaspoonfuls onto waxed paper. Cool before serving.

3 dozen

PINK DIVINITY

---

3 cups sugar
¾ cup light corn syrup
¾ cup hot water
¼ teaspoon salt
½ 3-ounce package cherry gelatin
2 egg whites, beaten until stiff but not dry
1 teaspoon vanilla extract
1 cup chopped nuts (*optional*)

෫෧ In 2-quart saucepan, combine sugar, corn syrup, water, and salt. Cook and stir over medium heat until sugar dissolves and mixture comes to a boil. Reduce heat to medium-low, and continue cooking until mixture comes to hard ball stage (260° F.), stirring only occasionally. Meanwhile, add gelatin powder to egg whites; stir in vanilla. Gradually pour syrup over egg whites, beating at high speed on electric mixer until candy holds its shape (4 to 5 minutes). Quickly stir in nuts and drop from teaspoon onto waxed paper.

About 40 pieces

Orange Junius

1¾ cups milk
½ pint (*1 cup*) vanilla ice cream
½ can (*⅓ cup*) frozen orange juice concentrate
1 teaspoon non-dairy creamer powder

ટ⌣ Combine all ingredients in electric blender or mixing bowl. Blend or beat with electric beater until smooth and almost fluffy. Pour into glasses and serve immediately.

4 servings

Apple Tea

---

1 12-ounce can frozen apple juice concentrate
3 juice cans water
2 tablespoons instant tea powder
1 tablespoon honey
½ teaspoon cinnamon
⅛ teaspoon nutmeg
Apple brandy (*optional*)

ટ⌣ In large saucepan or heat-proof teapot, combine juice concentrate and water; stir. Add tea, honey, cinnamon, and nutmeg. Heat through but do not boil. If you wish to add brandy, stir ½ to 1 jigger in each cup of hot tea.

8 servings

Dinner

TIME IS THE MOST VALUABLE THING
A MAN CAN SPEND

—Theophrastus

SHERRIED CLAM DIP

---

1 7½-ounce can minced clams, drained
2 cups commercial sour cream or 1 cup commercial sour
      cream and 1 cup yogurt
1 1½-ounce package dry spaghetti sauce mix
2 tablespoons sherry or vermouth (*optional*)
¼ teaspoon instant parsley flakes

ᔑ In blender or mixing bowl, blend all ingredients until almost smooth, being careful not to pulverize the clams. Let stand at least 20 minutes, for full flavor, then place in refrigerator. Serve chilled.   *2 cups*

DIETERS' DELIGHT DIP

---

2 cups cream-style cottage cheese
1 tablespoon sliced pimiento
1 teaspoon instant parsley flakes
1 envelope dill dip mix
1 tablespoon taco seasoning mix (*shake package before
      opening*)

ᔑ Blend all ingredients in blender or mixing bowl. Let stand at least 20 minutes for full flavor, then place in refrigerator. Serve chilled as dip for cooked shrimp, Brussels sprouts, or artichokes, raw carrots, celery sticks, zucchini slices, or cauliflowerettes.   *2 cups*

CHIDDINGSTONE CREAM
CHEESE SPREAD

---

1 3-ounce package cream cheese
½ cup bottled chutney or smooth chutney sauce*
1 tablespoon imitation bacon bits

ટ✦ Place cream cheese on small plate or in bowl. Cover with chutney or chutney sauce; sprinkle with bacon bits. Serve with sesame crackers or melba toast.

4 to 5 servings

* The chutney sauce is a bit more manageable.

FRENCH BREAD

---

2 8-ounce packages refrigerated country-style biscuits
1 egg white
1 tablespoon water

ટ✦ Preheat oven to 350° F. Lightly grease a cookie sheet. Open packages of biscuits, following directions on package, but do *not* separate biscuits. Place rolls of biscuits end to end, then gently press them together and flatten ends to form a loaf. Place on cookie sheet. In cup, combine and lightly beat egg white and water; brush on top and sides of loaf. Bake 30 minutes, or until golden brown. (Poppy seeds can be sprinkled on top for variety.)

1 loaf

Fish Fillets in Beer Batter

---

2 1-pound packages frozen fish fillets (*sole, haddock, perch, halibut, or cod*)
1 cup packaged pancake mix
1 to 1¼ cups beer
Shortening or cooking oil
Parsley flakes or paprika

ટ≈ Thaw fillets enough to separate; then cut into serving-size pieces. In pie plate, combine and mix pancake mix and beer. In skillet, heat ¼ inch shortening or oil. Dip fillets in batter and sauté, skin side up, until brown and almost crisp on one side. (Because these fillets have a tendency to stick to the pan, attention is needed in frying them.) Turn; brown other side until fish flakes easily with the point of a knife. After frying, drain fish immediately on paper towels to remove excess fat. Sprinkle with parsley flakes or paprika.

6 servings

Parslied Fish Fillets

---

2 1-pound packages frozen fish fillets (*sole, flounder, perch, or halibut*)
1 10-ounce can frozen shrimp or lobster bisque soup, partially thawed
1 10-ounce can condensed cream of mushroom soup
⅓ to ½ cup sherry or rosé wine or chicken consommé
1 tablespoon instant parsley flakes
Salt
Pepper or lemon pepper

ે Thaw fillets enough to separate; then cut into serving-size pieces. Preheat oven to 375° F. Butter large flat baking dish. Wipe fillets with damp cloth; place in prepared dish. In medium-sized saucepan, combine and heat soups over medium heat; stir to blend to smooth consistency. Do not boil. Stir in wine or consommé; pour over fish. Sprinkle with parsley flakes, and salt and pepper to taste. Bake 30 minutes, or until fish flakes easily at the point of a knife. Avoid overcooking.

6 servings

Fish Sticks Diavolo Magnifico

---

1 1-pound package frozen precooked fish sticks*
1 1½-ounce package dry spaghetti sauce mix
1 4-ounce package (*1 cup*) shredded pizza cheese
3 tablespoons grated Parmesan cheese

ֶ∾ Preheat oven to 400° F. Place fish sticks in flat baking dish; set aside. In saucepan, prepare spaghetti sauce mix, following directions on package, but using ½ the amount of water called for, and heat only to boiling point. Pour heated sauce over fish sticks. Sprinkle with cheeses. Bake 15 minutes, or until bubbly and well heated through.

4 servings

    * Clam sticks may be used.

Baked Haddock Fillets

---

2 1-pound packages frozen haddock fillets (*turbot, cod, bass, whiting, or shrimp may be used, also*)
¼ cup (*½ stick*) butter or margarine or cooking oil
1 egg, beaten lightly
½ cup milk
1½ cups instant mashed potato flakes
1 teaspoon lemon pepper
1 teaspoon salt

ᔥ Thaw fillets enough to separate; then cut into serving-size pieces. Preheat oven to 375° F. Place butter or margarine in large flat baking dish in oven to melt. In small bowl, beat together egg and milk. Place potato flakes in separate flat bowl. Dip fillets in milk mixture, then in potato flakes. Place coated fillets in melted butter in baking dish. Sprinkle with leftover potato flakes, leftover milk mixture, pepper, and salt. Bake 20 to 30 minutes, dotting with additional butter during baking if you wish. When done edges of fish become browned and crusty, and fish flakes easily at the point of a knife. Do not turn during cooking. Serve fish in same baking dish in which it has been cooked.

6 servings

Truites en Papillotes
(*Trout in Foil Wrapping*)

---

6 fresh or frozen and thawed trout (*8 to 10 ounces each*)
1 large onion, finely chopped
1 large carrot, finely chopped
2 tomatoes, cut into thirds
1 8- or 10-ounce bottle creamy French dressing
Heavy-duty aluminum foil

ᔒ If using fresh fish, cut head and tail off each trout. Holding trout by top of spine, gently loosen spine with small sharp knife or fingertip. Pull spine and bones free down the back to the tail and remove. Lay trout, opened flat, skin side down, on cookie sheet or large flat baking dish. Arrange onion and carrot on trout. Place tomato piece on each, and cover all with dressing. Marinate 20 minutes. With spatula, carefully remove each trout and place on individual sheet of double-thickness aluminum foil. Wrap closed, folding twice and twisting ends tightly. Bake at 350° F. for 20 to 30 minutes, or grill over glowing gray charcoal until done as desired. Serve in wrapping.

6 servings

Trout with Mushrooms

---

6 fresh or frozen and thawed trout (*8 to 10 ounces each*)
6 green onions, sliced
1 6-ounce can broiled-in-butter sliced mushrooms
½ teaspoon instant beef bouillon granules
½ cup boiling water
¼ cup white wine
½ teaspoon salt
¼ teaspoon lemon pepper

ౙ Butter large flat baking dish. In bottom, arrange onions, then trout, and mushrooms. In small bowl, combine bouillon granules and boiling water; stir to dissolve completely. Stir in wine, salt, and pepper. Pour over fish. Bake at 375° F. for 30 minutes, or until fish is tender.

6 servings

Baked Pecan Chicken

---

1 2½- to 3-pound broiler-fryer chicken, cut into pieces
1 cup packaged biscuit mix
½ cup chopped or broken pecans
1 teaspoon paprika
1 teaspoon salt
1 teaspoon poultry seasoning
1 cup commercial sour cream or ½ cup evaporated milk
½ cup (*1 stick*) melted butter or margarine

ɞ Preheat oven to 400° F. Grease shallow baking pan. Wash and pat dry chicken pieces. In flat dish, combine and mix biscuit mix, pecans, paprika, salt, and poultry seasoning. With rubber spatula or broad knife, spread sour cream over chicken pieces or coat with evaporated milk, then roll in biscuit mix. Place chicken pieces, skin side up, not touching, in prepared baking pan. Sprinkle with any remaining mix and drizzle with butter. Bake 40 minutes, or until tender. Do not turn.

4 servings

BAKED CHICKEN SESAME

---

1 2½- to 3-pound broiler-fryer chicken, cut into pieces
1 envelope green onion dip mix
½ cup (*1 stick*) butter or margarine, softened
1 teaspoon paprika
1 cup packaged cornflake crumbs or crushed stuffing mix
2 tablespoons sesame seeds

ଓ Preheat oven to 400° F. Butter large shallow baking dish. Wash and completely pat dry chicken pieces. In small bowl, blend dip mix, butter or margarine, and paprika to a paste with wooden spoon. With rubber spatula or broad knife, spread mixture over chicken pieces, then roll in crumbs. Place chicken pieces, skin side up, not touching, in prepared pan. Sprinkle with sesame seeds. Bake 40 minutes, or until tender. Do not turn.

4 servings

BAKED CHICKEN BREASTS ROQUEFORT

---

3 chicken breasts, cut in half
¾ cup bottled Italian-style dressing
¾ cup bottled Roquefort or blue cheese dressing
¼ cup packaged cornflake crumbs
1 tablespoon instant parsley flakes

᳕ Preheat oven to 375° F. Wash and pat dry chicken breasts. Place in shallow baking pan, and pour Italian-style dressing over chicken. Marinate 10 minutes, turning to coat all sides. Bake 30 minutes. Remove from oven. Cover with Roquefort or blue cheese dressing; sprinkle with crumbs and parsley flakes. Bake 15 minutes more, or until chicken is golden and tender.

6 servings

HURRY CURRY
(*Chicken Curry*)

½ cup chopped onion
2 tablespoons butter
1 10½-ounce can condensed cream of mushroom soup
¼ cup milk
1 cup commercial sour cream
1 to 1½ teaspoons curry powder
2 tablespoons coconut syrup or ½ cup chopped apple
    (*optional*)
1 7-ounce package (2 *cups*) frozen cooked and diced
    chicken
Chopped parsley

ح‍‍و In skillet, sauté onion in melted butter until limp. Add soup and milk; stir. Add sour cream and curry powder to soup mixture; heat and stir until smooth. Add coconut syrup or apple, and chicken; heat through, but do not allow to boil. Serve over hot cooked rice, garnished with parsley.

4 to 6 servings

Chicken Hong Kong

---

1 10½-ounce can condensed cream of mushroom soup
½ cup half-and-half cream
1 teaspoon salt
1½ 7-ounce packages (*3 cups*) frozen cooked and diced
    chicken
2 9-ounce packages frozen French-style green beans,
    thawed
1 14½-ounce can chop suey vegetables, drained
1 teaspoon instant minced onion
1½ 4-ounce packages (*1½ cups*) shredded Cheddar
    cheese
1 3½-ounce can French fried onion rings

𝔷𝔴 Preheat oven to 350° F. Butter 12 × 7½ × 2-inch ovenproof baking dish. In large bowl, combine soup, cream, and salt; stir until smooth. Add chicken, beans, chop suey vegetables, minced onion, and cheese; toss lightly to mix. Spoon into prepared baking dish. Bake 40 minutes, or until beans are tender. Top with onion rings; bake 10 to 15 minutes more, or until onion rings are heated through and casserole is bubbly and done.

6 to 8 servings

CONTEMPORARY CASSOULET

---

2 tablespoons salad or cooking oil
¾ pound Italian-style link sausage, cut into 1-inch pieces
1 medium onion, chopped
1 6-ounce can tomato sauce
1 1-pound can Italian pear tomatoes
1 green pepper, seeded and cut into 1-inch pieces
2 1-pound cans white kidney or great northern beans
¼ teaspoon hot pepper sauce
1 teaspoon salt
½ cup dry white wine
1 32-ounce package frozen cooked and breaded chicken
   (*10 pieces*)
1 cup packaged soup-and-salad croutons
1 tablespoon instant parsley flakes

౭∾ Preheat oven to 350° F. Heat oil in Dutch oven or large deep skillet with cover. Add sausage pieces and onion; cook over medium heat until onion is transparent and sausage is browned. Pour off excess fat, or transfer sausage and onion to large ovenproof casserole with cover. Add tomato sauce, tomatoes, green pepper, beans, hot pepper sauce, and salt; stir to blend flavors. Add wine; stir again. Arrange chicken pieces on bean mixture. Cover. Bake 15 minutes. Meanwhile, in closed paper bag, crush croutons with rolling pin; mix in parsley flakes. Sprinkle over cassoulet, then use wooden spoon to push crumbs partially into pan juices. Bake 25 minutes more, or until chicken pieces are completely heated through and sauce is bubbly. Serve directly from cooking pot.

4 servings

BEEF SINGAPORE

---

2 pounds top round steak, cut into paper-thin slices
Non-seasoned meat tenderizer
¼ cup cooking oil
1 tablespoon instant minced onion
½ cup soy sauce
3 tablespoons brown sugar
2 green peppers, seeded and cut into strips
1 1-pound 14½-ounce can pineapple chunks, drained
1 teaspoon ginger powder

ᔆᔜ Sprinkle meat with tenderizer, following directions on label. In large skillet, quickly brown meat on all sides in hot oil. Sprinkle with onion. Add remaining ingredients. Cover, and heat through, about 10 minutes. Serve over hot buttered rice.

6 servings

Meat Loaf Senegalese

---

1 pound ground lamb
1 pound lean ground beef
1 tablespoon imitation bacon bits
2 cups packaged herb-seasoned stuffing croutons
¼ cup flaked coconut
¼ cup golden seedless raisins
¼ cup chopped chutney
1 egg, beaten
½ 6-ounce can curry seasoning or curry sauce
1 teaspoon salt

℞ Preheat oven to 375° F. Combine all ingredients in large mixing bowl. Toss lightly but well. Spoon mixture into 8-inch square baking dish. Bake 30 to 45 minutes, or until done. Serve with chutney, or Chutney-Chili Sauce, if desired.   *6 servings*

Chutney-Chili Sauce

---

1 cup bottled chili sauce
½ cup bottled chutney
1 teaspoon instant minced onion
½ teaspoon salt
¼ teaspoon garlic powder (*not garlic salt*)

℞ In bowl, blend all ingredients together with a wooden spoon or rubber spatula. Let stand at least 10 minutes before using.   *1½ cups*

Tasty Hasty Stew
(*15-Minute Stew*)

1½ pounds cubed steak, cut into 1½-inch pieces
Flour
2 tablespoons cooking oil
1 envelope sloppy joe or goulash seasoning mix
1 1-pound can whole carrots with juice
1 1-pound can diced Irish potatoes with juice
1 1-pound can whole small white onions with juice
1 8-ounce can tomato sauce
1 teaspoon Worcestershire sauce
2 tablespoons sherry or madeira

ಶಿ Dust meat with flour. In heavy Dutch oven, skillet, or electric skillet, brown meat in hot oil. Add seasoning mix and stir; then add carrots, potatoes, onions, tomato sauce, and Worcestershire sauce. Heat through. Stir in wine. Cover; simmer 5 to 10 minutes.

6 servings

STEAK DIANE

---

6 cubed steaks, cut ½-inch thick*
Non-seasoned meat tenderizer (*optional*)
Salt
Lemon pepper or seasoned pepper
2 teaspoons mustard powder
6 tablespoons butter or margarine
2 tablespoons freeze-dried chives
1 teaspoon instant parsley flakes
Juice of ½ large lemon
2 teaspoons Worcestershire sauce

ह॰ Have butcher tenderize and pound steaks *very* thin. Sprinkle steaks with tenderizer, salt and pepper to taste; and 1 teaspoon mustard powder. Press seasonings into steaks with fingers or spatula. Turn and repeat on other side. Melt butter or margarine in skillet, electric skillet, or chafing dish. Sauté steaks 2 to 4 minutes on one side. Sprinkle with chives, parsley flakes, lemon juice, and Worcestershire sauce. Turn; sauté 2 to 4 minutes on other side, or until done as desired. Remove to heated serving platter. Pour pan juices over steaks when serving.   *6 servings*

* Sirloin strip steaks may be used.

LAMB PATTIES WITH DILL SAUCE

1½ pounds ground lamb
  1 envelope instant oatmeal
  1 egg, beaten
  1 tablespoon instant minced onion
  ¾ teaspoon salt or seasoning salt
  ¼ teaspoon powdered thyme
Freshly ground pepper
  6 slices bacon
Dill Sauce (*below*)
Grated Parmesan cheese

ह≫ In bowl, combine lamb, oatmeal, egg, onion, salt, thyme, and pepper to taste. Toss lightly but well. Shape into 6 patties. Wrap a bacon slice around each patty and secure with toothpick. Broil 5 inches from heat for 10 minutes; turn and broil 5 minutes more. Or pan-fry or charcoal grill until done to taste. Serve with Dill Sauce, and sprinkle with cheese.   *6 servings*

DILL SAUCE

---

  1 1¼-ounce package sour cream sauce mix
  ¼ cup milk
  ¼ cup half-and-half cream
  1 teaspoon dried dill weed

ह≫ In small bowl, combine sour cream sauce mix, milk, and cream. Stir until smooth. Stir in dill. Allow to stand 10 minutes, or cover and refrigerate until needed. This sauce is also good with chicken, fish, zucchini, and green or lima beans.   *2 cups*

Baked Lemon Lamb Chops

---

1 tablespoon buttery-type oil
6 round bone shoulder lamb chops, cut ½-inch thick, trimmed of fat
6 thin slices onion
1 1-pound 7-ounce can instant lemon filling for pies
½ cup water
⅓ cup white vinegar
¼ cup soy sauce
Salt
Lemon pepper
Instant dried parsley

ঌ Preheat oven to 350° F. In skillet, heat oil. Quickly brown chops on both sides. Remove to ovenproof baking dish large enough to accommodate chops in single layer. Place onion slice on each chop. In medium-sized bowl, combine remaining ingredients except parsley. Stir or beat with wire whisk until smooth. Spoon or pour over chops. Cover. Bake 45 minutes; remove cover, bake 15 minutes more, or until chops are fork tender. Sprinkle with parsley.

6 servings

VEAL VERMOUTH

2½ pounds veal cutlets, cut into ¾-inch thick pieces
Flour
Olive, buttery-type, or cooking oil
 ½ cup bottled Italian-style dressing
 1 4-ounce can broiled-in-butter sliced mushrooms
 ⅓ cup dry vermouth
Grated Parmesan cheese

&~ Dust veal pieces with flour. In large skillet, heat oil and quickly brown meat on both sides. Pour dressing into skillet around cutlets; cover, and simmer 20 minutes. Add mushrooms and vermouth. Heat through. To serve, spoon pan juices over meat, then sprinkle with cheese.

6 servings

CEYLON PORK CHOP BAKE

---

6 pork or veal loin chops, cut 1-inch thick
Salt
Lemon pepper
1 tablespoon buttery-type oil
½ cup white wine, chicken broth, or water
1 teaspoon instant tea powder
2 tablespoons ketchup
1 1-pound can whole small onions

ဦ Sprinkle chops with salt and lemon pepper. In large skillet heat oil, and quickly brown chops on both sides. In small saucepan, heat wine, broth, or water; add tea and ketchup. Pour over browned chops. Add onions. Cover. Bake at 350° F. for 40 minutes, or until tender and done.

6 servings

PINEAPPLE PORK CHOPS

---

6 center cut pork chops, cut ¾-inch thick, or 2 pounds
　　pork cutlets
1 6-ounce can frozen pineapple juice concentrate
2 tablespoons brown sugar, firmly packed
¼ cup wine vinegar
¼ cup honey

➢ Trim all fat off meat. Combine remaining ingredients in small bowl; mix until blended, as sauce may be a bit stiff. Place chops or cutlets on bottom of broiler pan, using no rack. Brush with sauce. Broil at lowest heat, or on lowest oven rack, 15 minutes. Turn, brush with sauce, broil 15 minutes more, or until done. Brush frequently with sauce during cooking, and again just before serving.

6 servings

East Indian Ribs

---

3 to 4 pounds spareribs or country-style ribs
1 1-pound 6-ounce can instant apricot-pineapple filling
    for pies
Juice of 1 lemon
¼ cup water
1 to 2 tablespoons curry powder
1 teaspoon salt
½ teaspoon ginger powder
¼ cup sherry (*optional*)

ᔖ Preheat oven to 350° F. Place ribs on rack of broiler pan, meaty side up. Bake 30 minutes. Remove from oven. Drain off fat. Meanwhile, combine remaining ingredients in saucepan; stir and heat until bubbly, reduce heat, and simmer 4 to 5 minutes. Spoon on ribs. Bake ribs 40 minutes longer, or until done. Sauce will form a glaze during baking.

6 servings

Liver with White Wine

---

1 pound calves liver, sliced
Flour
¼ cup olive oil or butter, or half of each
2 cloves garlic, cut in half and speared onto toothpick
1 small onion, minced
Ground white pepper or seasoned pepper
¾ teaspoon crumbled sweet basil
½ cup dry sherry
½ cup imitation bacon bits

ş❧ Wipe liver with a damp cloth or paper towel; dredge in flour. In skillet, quickly brown liver on both sides in oil or melted butter. Remove liver to heated platter. In same skillet, brown garlic and onion 5 minutes, or until onion is limp. Return liver to pan; sprinkle with pepper to taste and sweet basil. Add wine. Cover; simmer over low heat 20 minutes, or until tender, basting often with pan juices. Discard garlic, and serve liver sprinkled with bacon bits.

4 to 5 servings

Brussels Sprouts Caraway

2 10-ounce packages frozen Brussels sprouts
6 tablespoons butter
1 tablespoon caraway seeds
2 tablespoons packaged cornflake or fine dry bread crumbs
Few drops dry vermouth

ౢ∾ Cook Brussels sprouts, following directions on package; drain. Stir in butter and caraway seeds. Sprinkle lightly with crumbs, dot with additional butter and vermouth. *6 servings*

Curried Onions

1 12-ounce package frozen diced or chopped onions
4 tablespoons butter, margarine, or salad oil
1 teaspoon curry powder
¾ teaspoon salt
½ teaspoon seasoned pepper or lemon pepper

ౢ∾ In skillet, sauté onions in butter, margarine, or oil, until limp and golden (about 10 minutes), breaking them apart with wooden spoon. Stir in remaining ingredients. Cook 3 to 4 minutes more, or until flavors are completely blended and onions are no longer raw. *4 to 6 servings*

SILKEN SQUASH CASSEROLE

---

2 14-ounce packages frozen mashed cooked squash
¾ cup canned dietetic applesauce
Salt
Pepper or lemon pepper
⅓ cup packaged cornflake crumbs
2 tablespoons brown sugar
1 tablespoon rum (*optional*)
Butter

꿈 Preheat oven to 350° F. Butter 1½-quart casserole. Cook squash in saucepan, following directions on package. Add applesauce, and salt and pepper to taste. Spoon into prepared casserole. In small bowl, mix crumbs, sugar, and rum. Sprinkle over top of squash. Dot with butter. Bake 15 minutes, or until well heated through and crumbs are golden.

6 to 8 servings

Spinach Rarebit

---

2 10-ounce packages frozen chopped spinach
1 5-ounce can thinly sliced water chestnuts, drained
1 10-ounce package frozen Welsh rarebit, thawed
2 tablespoons imitation bacon bits
Ground nutmeg
1 5-ounce package frozen French fried onion rings

ৡ᠉ Preheat oven to 350° F. Generously butter 8-inch square baking dish. Prepare spinach in saucepan, following directions on package; drain thoroughly. Spread spinach on bottom of prepared dish. Top with water chestnuts and rarebit. Sprinkle with bacon bits and nutmeg; top with onion rings. Bake 15 to 20 minutes, or until well heated through.

6 servings

Eggplant Roquefort *

---

1 medium eggplant (*1½ pounds*)
½ cup bottled Roquefort dressing
½ cup packaged cornflake crumbs
¼ cup olive or salad oil, or half of each

ह❧ Peel eggplant and slice lengthwise. Dip slices in dressing, then in crumbs. Heat oil in large skillet; add eggplant. Cook uncovered over medium heat until tender and golden brown on bottom side; turn with spatula and cook other side.

4 to 6 servings

* This can also be made with 3 medium zucchini, about ½ pound each.

Novel Succotash

---

1 10-ounce package frozen succotash
1 teaspoon seasoning salt
1 tablespoon instant sweet pepper flakes
½ 10-ounce package frozen peas
½ cup packaged soup-and-salad croutons
2 tablespoons melted butter or margarine, or buttery-
    type cooking oil

In medium-sized saucepan, cook succotash following directions on package, but using seasoning salt and
adding pepper flakes. Add peas 2 or 3 minutes before end
of cooking time. Drain well. Meanwhile, in small skillet,
sauté croutons in butter, margarine, or oil. Sprinkle over
succotash, then toss lightly.   *4 to 5 servings*

Cole Slaw Sonora

---

1 8-ounce package (*4 cups*) cole slaw mixture
1½ cups commercial sour cream
1 tablespoon wine vinegar
1 tablespoon celery seed
1 teaspoon sugar
½ teaspoon instant parsley flakes
1 cup frozen and thawed, or canned pineapple chunks,
    drained

Rinse cole slaw; shake or pat dry. In small bowl,
combine and blend remaining ingredients. In salad bowl,
combine slaw and dressing; toss lightly but well.

4 to 5 servings

Apple Gratine

---

2 1-pound 5-ounce cans instant apple filling for pies
½ teaspoon nutmeg
1 teaspoon cinnamon
1 8-ounce package refrigerated quick crescent dinner rolls
1 cup commercial sour cream
1 3-ounce package cream cheese, softened
1 cup brown sugar, firmly packed

₷ᴖ Preheat oven to 375° F. Butter 13 × 9 × 2-inch baking dish. Place apple filling in bottom of dish; sprinkle with nutmeg and cinnamon. Unroll dough; separate into 8 triangles. Arrange on top of apples. (Dough will not completely cover apples.) In medium-sized bowl, combine sour cream, cream cheese, and sugar; blend until smooth. Spread over dough. Bake 30 minutes. Serve warm or cold. Gratiné may be topped with whipped cream or topping, or with cream.

8 servings

Peach Cobbler

---

1 1-pound 5-ounce can instant peach filling for pies
¼ cup water
1 tablespoon lemon juice
1 11.9-ounce package refrigerated orange Danish rolls
with icing

ટ৯   Preheat oven to 400° F. Butter 8¼ × 1¾-inch round ovenproof cake dish. In saucepan, heat pie filling, water, and lemon juice, but do not allow to boil. Pour hot pie filling into prepared dish; top with rolls, cut side up. Bake 15 minutes, or until rolls are golden. Remove from oven; ice with package icing while warm.   *8 servings*

Blackberry Cookie Cobbler

---

1 1-pound 6-ounce can instant blackberry filling for pies
1 15.3-ounce package refrigerated butterscotch-nut slice-
and-bake cookies

ટ৯   Preheat oven to 375° F. Pour pie filling into 8¼ × 1¾-inch round ovenproof cake dish. Cut cookie dough into slices, about ⅓-inch thick. Place on top of pie filling. Bake on middle shelf of oven for 10 minutes, or until cookie topping is done. Serve warm. (If there is any leftover cookie dough, use it for cookies.)   *6 servings*

Grapes Creme de Cacao

---

3 cups seedless green or Tokay grapes
½ cup commercial sour cream
Brown sugar
Crème de cacao
Instant grated orange peel

ϡ   Wash and drain grapes. (Remove seeds from Tokay grapes.) Chill. When ready to serve, place grapes in mixing bowl, add sour cream and toss lightly but enough to coat grapes. Spoon into sherbet glasses or dessert dishes. Sprinkle each serving with brown sugar, crème de cacao, and orange peel to taste. Serve chilled.   *6 servings*

Cherries Jubilee Instante

---

1 1-pound 5-ounce can instant cherry filling for pies
¼ to ½ cup cherry brandy or light rum
¼ cup water
1 quart vanilla, French vanilla, or cherry vanilla ice cream

ϡ   In skillet, saucepan, or chafing dish, combine cherry filling, brandy or rum, and water. Heat through, but do not boil; simmer 2 minutes. Spoon over ice cream.

To serve flaming: heat cherry filling and brandy or rum separately. Pour heated brandy or rum over cherries; ignite. Spoon over ice cream.   *8 servings*

TRUFFLES

1¾ cups semi-sweet chocolate bits
 2 tablespoons water
 1 cup powdered sugar
 ⅓ cup whipping cream
 2 tablespoons light rum or 1 teaspoon vanilla extract
 2 tablespoons cocoa or chocolate decorettes

ॐ Butter sides and bottom of top of double boiler. In it combine chocolate bits and water. Cook over simmering water, stirring occasionally, until chocolate is melted. Pour into medium-sized bowl. Stir in powdered sugar, cream, and rum or vanilla; beat very well. Cover with sheet of waxed paper, placing paper directly on chocolate mixture, to prevent top from hardening. Refrigerate 1 hour. Shape chocolate mixture into little balls; roll in cocoa or decorettes. Cover and store in cool place or in refrigerator.

About 3 dozen balls

Guest

MANKIND IS DIVISIBLE

INTO TWO GREAT CLASSES:

HOSTS AND GUESTS.

—Max Beerbohm

Brunch

IF YOU LOSE AN HOUR IN THE MORNING,
YOU HAVE TO HUNT FOR IT
THE REST OF THE DAY.

—Chinese Proverb

Breakfast Treats Monsieur

---

1 12-ounce can luncheon meat
½ cup packaged cornflake crumbs
1 15½-ounce can pineapple slices, drained
Butter
1 teaspoon instant parsley flakes

ટ✖ Butter large flat baking dish or cookie sheet. Cut luncheon meat into 8 slices. Dip into crumbs, covering both sides. Place meat slices in prepared dish. Cover with pineapple slices. Dot with butter. Sprinkle with parsley and any remaining crumbs. Bake at 350° F. for 20 minutes.

4 double servings

MEAT AND SPINACH OMELET

---

1 10-ounce package frozen chopped spinach
¼ cup (½ *stick*) butter
1 cup frozen diced onion
1 pound lean ground beef
1 4-ounce can sliced mushrooms, drained
Salt
Pepper or seasoned pepper
Garlic salt
6 eggs, beaten
1 teaspoon Worcestershire sauce

੭ᵛ Cook spinach, following directions on package; drain well. Melt butter in large skillet. Add onions; cook over medium heat until onions are golden and limp. Add beef; cook until browned, chopping beef into small granules as it cooks. Stir in spinach, mushrooms, and salt, pepper, and garlic salt to taste. Pour in eggs and Worcestershire sauce. Cook, stirring lightly until eggs are almost set. Use spatula to turn, and continue cooking until eggs are cooked through.

4 to 6 servings

Egg Flan Gourmandise

---

1 9-inch packaged frozen unbaked pie shell
4 eggs
1 package (*1 cup*) chicken gravy mix
1 to 3 teaspoons sherry (*optional*)
1 6-ounce can broiled-in-butter chopped or sliced mushrooms

ཚ *To prepare flan crust:* Preheat oven to 375° F. Allow pie shell to thaw 10 to 15 minutes in pie tin. Place
crust on underneath side of pie tin; perforate with fork
several times. Place in center of oven on cookie sheet. Bake
15 minutes, or until golden. (Meanwhile, poach eggs; keep
them warm.)

To assemble flan: Prepare gravy in small saucepan, following directions on package. Stir in sherry; keep warm.
Replace baked pastry inside pie tin. Arrange layer of mushrooms with juices in bottom of pie shell. Arrange poached
eggs over mushrooms. Pour gravy mixture over and around
eggs. Heat through in oven for 5 minutes. Serve warm.

4 servings

BAKED EGGS FROMAGE

---

1 4-ounce package (*1 cup*) shredded Cheddar or American cheese
1 teaspoon instant minced onion
6 eggs
½ teaspoon salt
¼ teaspoon seasoned pepper

ဆာ Preheat oven to 400° F. Generously butter shallow baking dish. In small bowl, toss together ¾ cup cheese and onion. Spread on bottom of prepared dish. Break eggs, one at a time, into cup, then slide onto cheese. Sprinkle with salt and pepper, then remaining cheese. Bake about 20 minutes, or until eggs are done to taste. Do not overbake, as eggs continue cooking when removed from oven.

6 servings

WAKE-UP BISCUIT BASKETS
(*Eggs Baked in Pastry*)

---

1 8-ounce package refrigerated biscuits
6 eggs
Salt
Pepper
Thyme, rosemary, or chervil (*optional*)
Shredded Cheddar cheese

ह∾ Preheat oven to 400° F. Generously butter 6 custard or muffin pan cups. On floured board, roll out 6 biscuits, each into a 5- or 6-inch circle. Place each circle in
a muffin pan cup, fitting dough to sides and bottom.
Break eggs, one at a time, into cup, then slide into a
dough-lined cup. Sprinkle with salt and pepper and herbs
to taste. Bake 15 to 20 minutes, or until done as desired.
Sprinkle tops with cheese just a few minutes before they
are through baking.

6 servings

SOUFFLE JAMBON
(*Ham Soufflé*)

¼ cup packaged cornflake crumbs
1 10½-ounce (*1¼ cups*) can white sauce
1 teaspoon salt or seasoning salt
¼ teaspoon pepper
1 teaspoon prepared mustard
½ teaspoon crumbled sweet basil (*optional*)
6 egg yolks
7 egg whites
1½ cups cooked diced ham*

૨∾ Preheat oven to 350° F. Generously butter a 2-quart soufflé dish or straight-side ovenproof casserole. Coat buttered surface with cornflake crumbs. In small saucepan, combine white sauce, salt, pepper, mustard, and sweet basil; heat, stirring to blend, but do not boil. Meanwhile, in large mixing bowl, beat egg yolks lightly; set aside. In medium-sized mixing bowl, beat egg whites until stiff, but not dry; set aside. Add a little hot white sauce to egg yolks, blend; add remaining white sauce to yolks and mix. Fold in egg whites and ham. Carefully pour mixture into prepared dish. Bake 25 to 35 minutes, or until set and center of soufflé does not shake when moved. Top will be golden. Serve immediately.   *6 servings*

* Cooked shrimp, crab, chicken, or cheese may be used.

Undercover Sausages

---

1 8-ounce package brown-and-serve sausages
1 8-ounce package refrigerated biscuits
Half-and-half cream
Poppy seeds (*optional*)

ૐ❧   Preheat oven to 400° F. Place sausages in shallow pan. Bake 5 minutes; remove from oven; drain on paper toweling. On lightly floured board, roll out each biscuit into a 4- or 5-inch oblong. Place a sausage at tip of each biscuit, and roll up jelly-roll fashion, allowing ends of sausage to peek out of dough. Place seam-side down on ungreased cookie sheet. Brush tops with cream for golden color. Sprinkle with poppy seeds. Bake 10 minutes, or until done.   *10 rolls*

Holiday Pancakes

---

2 cups packaged pound cake mix (*shake package before opening*)
1⅓ cups milk
2 eggs
6 tablespoons melted butter or margarine

᠌ Preheat pancake griddle, skillet, or electric frying pan. In large mixing bowl, combine all ingredients and mix until quite smooth. Lightly grease griddle. Pour or spoon batter onto hot cooking surface, making pancakes in desired size. Cook until pancake top is covered with bubbles and edges look cooked. Turn and cook other side. Roll each pancake up jelly-roll style and top with prepared whipped topping, fresh fruit, powdered sugar, Orange Syrup, page 11, or Whipped Ginger Topping, page 14.

Batter to serve 4 to 6

Pumpkin Muffins

---

2 cups packaged biscuit mix
½ cup sugar
¼ teaspoon cinnamon
⅛ teaspoon allspice
⅛ teaspoon nutmeg
¾ cup milk
½ cup canned pumpkin
1 egg, beaten
2 tablespoons cooking oil

ello> Preheat oven to 400° F. Grease 2-inch muffin pan cups. In medium-sized mixing bowl, combine biscuit mix, sugar, cinnamon, allspice, and nutmeg. In small bowl, combine milk, pumpkin, eggs, and oil, stirring with spoon or whisk until well blended. Stir pumpkin mixture into dry ingredients, mixing until almost smooth. Fill muffin pan cups ⅔ full. Bake about 20 minutes, or until golden and done.

18 muffins

Swedish Jelly Buns

---

12 **brown-and-serve rolls**
 1 **12-ounce jar apricot or raspberry preserves**
 1 **cup sifted powdered sugar**
 2 **tablespoons milk**

ૐ⋗   Preheat oven to 350° F. Use spoon or melon-baller to scoop out a circle the size of a quarter from top of each roll. Fill hole with preserves. Place filled buns on ungreased cookie sheet. Bake 15 minutes. Meanwhile, in small bowl, combine sugar with milk to make glaze. Spoon glaze over baked hot rolls.   *12 buns*

English Tea Bread

---

 1 **8-ounce package refrigerated biscuits**
¼ **cup brown sugar**
¼ **cup chopped nuts**
 1 **tablespoon flour**
½ **teaspoon cinnamon**
 2 **tablespoons melted butter**
½ **cup packaged cornflake crumbs**

ૐ⋗   Preheat oven to 425° F. Generously butter 8-inch pie plate. Place biscuits, touching each other, in buttered pan. In small bowl, combine and mix remaining ingredients. Sprinkle on top of biscuits. Bake 10 to 12 minutes, or until done.   *1 round loaf*

Viennese Christmas Bread

3 cups packaged biscuit mix
½ cup sugar
½ teaspoon ground coriander
1 egg
1¼ cups milk
1 cup chopped or broken pecans
1 cup assorted cut-up gumdrops (*omit licorice*)

ફ Preheat oven to 350° F. Grease and line with waxed paper a 9 × 5 × 3-inch baking dish. In mixing bowl, combine biscuit mix, sugar, coriander, egg, and milk. Beat vigorously with mixer one-half minute, or by hand for 40 strokes (batter will be lumpy). Stir in nuts and gumdrops. Pour batter into prepared pan. Bake 50 to 60 minutes, or until golden on top and cake tester inserted in center comes out clean. Cool. Serve thin slices, for it is rich.

1 loaf

PANETTONE
(*Italian Cake*)

---

1 1-pound loaf frozen ready-to-bake Italian-style bread,
    softened*
⅓ cup dark seedless raisins
⅓ cup golden seedless raisins
1 4-ounce package (½ *cup*) candied pineapple, chopped
1 egg
1½ teaspoons cream or milk

ৡ৶   Line a 9 × 5 × 3-inch baking dish with waxed paper. On breadboard or in large bowl, mix softened dough with raisins and pineapple pieces; place in prepared dish. In small bowl, combine egg and milk; beat with fork until lightly blended. Brush over top of dough. Cover with damp cloth and let rise in warm place (90° to 150° F.) until doubled in bulk. (Exact time will depend on dampness and warmth of place.)

Preheat oven to 350° F. Use sharp knife to cut a cross on top of dough. Place small pan of water in oven, to help cake rise and make crust glossy. Bake 25 minutes, or until done. Cool on cake rack.   *1 loaf*

---

* Allow frozen bread to soften in refrigerator overnight or at room temperature about 1½ hours.

Luncheon

IT IS NOT THE QUANTITY OF THE MEAT,

BUT THE CHEERFULNESS OF THE GUESTS,

WHICH MAKES THE FEAST.

—Clarendon

Avocado Soup with Almonds

---

  1 2-ounce package instant mashed potatoes
1½ cups hot chicken broth
  1 teaspoon instant minced onion
2½ cups cold or room temperature chicken broth
  1 7¾-ounce can frozen avocado dip, thawed
1½ cups cream
Few drops hot pepper sauce
  1 teaspoon salt
 ¼ teaspoon pepper
Toasted slivered almonds

᨞ In medium-sized bowl, combine potatoes, hot broth, and onion; beat briskly with fork to blend. Place mixture in blender or mixing bowl. Add cold broth and avocado dip; blend until smooth. Pour into large mixing bowl, and stir in cream, hot pepper sauce, salt, and pepper. Serve cold garnished with few slices of almonds floating on top.

6 to 8 servings

CRAB BISQUE

---

1 10½-ounce can condensed cream of asparagus soup
1 10½-ounce can condensed cream of mushroom soup
2 soup cans milk or 1½ soup cans milk and ½ soup can
    white wine
1 cup half-and-half cream
1 6½- to 7½-ounce can (*1 cup*) crab meat, drained, picked
    over and flaked
2 tablespoons butter
Nutmeg
2 teaspoons instant parsley flakes

ટે◞ In heavy saucepan, blend soups with wire whisk or slotted spoon until quite smooth. Add milk and cream. Heat and stir until soup is just to boiling point. Cover; cook 2 minutes, but do not allow to boil. Add crab meat; heat through. Stir in butter. Serve with nutmeg and parsley flakes sprinkled over top.

6 servings

Acapulco Fruit Soup

---

1 12-ounce package frozen melon balls, partially thawed
4 tablespoons frozen Hawaiian Punch concentrate, partially thawed
4 tablespoons frozen daiquiri mix, partially thawed (*shake can before opening*)
½ large banana, sliced
2 tablespoons orange juice
1 tablespoon lime juice

ß∾ Whirl all ingredients in blender at medium speed until blended but not quite smooth. Serve in cantaloupe or coconut halves, or in stemmed sherbet glasses or small fruit dishes.

4 to 6 servings

Shrimp Aspic

1½ cups cooked chilled deveined shrimp
2 10½-ounce cans *chilled* beef consommé*
¼ teaspoon lemon pepper
½ teaspoon instant grated orange peel
2 tablespoons sherry
6 slices lime

Cut shrimp into ½-inch pieces. In bowl, combine and mix all ingredients except sherry and lime. Spoon into cups, dishes, or stemmed glasses. Sprinkle with sherry and garnish with lime slices.

6 servings

* Place in refrigerator the night before, or at least 4 hours before serving.

SHRIMP NEWBURG

2 10-ounce cans frozen condensed cream of shrimp soup
   or lobster Langostino bisque, thawed*
⅓ cup half-and-half cream
1 1-pound package individually frozen peeled and deveined shrimp
2 teaspoons lemon juice
4 egg yolks
¼ cup sherry
Few drops hot pepper sauce
Salt
Pepper
Nutmeg

క్త్ In heavy saucepan, slowly heat soup, cream, and
shrimp. (Shrimp will cook as soup warms through completely.) Add lemon juice; simmer 2 minutes. In bowl,
beat egg yolks with sherry. Add shrimp mixture to it gradually to prevent curdling. Season to taste with hot pepper
sauce, salt, pepper, and nutmeg. Transfer to chafing dish
to keep warm. Serve from chafing dish on patty shells, or
over rice or toast.   *6 servings*

   * Unopened can of frozen soup will thaw in 30 minutes if
placed in hot water.

Shrimp Fromage

---

1 1½-pound package individually frozen peeled and deveined shrimp
1 8-ounce package macaroni and Cheddar dinner
1 tablespoon butter
2 cups boiling water
½ cup white wine
½ 4-ounce package (½ *cup*) shredded Cheddar cheese
1 tablespoon instant minced onion
¼ teaspoon dried sweet basil
½ teaspoon instant parsley flakes
¼ cup packaged cornflake crumbs
1 tablespoon thick cream (*or additional butter*)

ড়৶ Preheat oven to 375° F. In 2½-quart casserole with
cover, combine all ingredients, except crumbs and cream;
stir to blend completely. Cover; bake 40 minutes, stirring
once or twice during cooking. Remove from oven; sprinkle
with crumbs and cream (or dot with butter). Bake 10
minutes more. Let stand 10 minutes before serving.

6 servings

CHICKEN BREASTS POLONAISE

---

1 10½-ounce can condensed cream of celery soup
1 10½-ounce can condensed cream of chicken soup
1 envelope onion soup mix
¼ cup water
¾ cup dry red wine
1 cup rice, uncooked
3 chicken breasts, boned, skinned, and cut in half
1 tablespoon grated Parmesan cheese
2 teaspoons instant parsley flakes

২ৡ Preheat oven to 350° F. In large bowl, combine soups, soup mix, water, wine, and rice. Pour or spoon into 3-quart ovenproof casserole with cover. Arrange chicken on top of rice mixture; cover. Bake 1 hour; stir, sprinkle with cheese and parsley flakes; re-cover and bake 1 hour more, or until chicken and rice are tender.

6 servings

Enchiladas Acapulco con Pollo

½ cup corn, soy, or vegetable oil
12 refrigerated, canned, or frozen and thawed corn tortillas
1 10-ounce can red chili sauce
1 7-ounce package (2 *cups*) frozen cooked and diced chicken
1 4½-ounce can (½ *cup*) chopped ripe olives
½ cup chopped almonds
2 4-ounce packages (2 *cups*) shredded Cheddar cheese
1 cup commercial sour cream
4 teaspoons minced scallions or green onions and tops

ౖ❧ Preheat oven to 350° F. In medium-sized skillet over medium heat, bring oil to hot but not smoking temperature. Dip each tortilla in hot oil for a second to soften it, turning with tongs so it will not break. Drain on paper toweling. Dip in chili sauce. In bowl, combine chicken, olives, almonds, and ½ cup cheese; toss to mix. Place large spoonful of chicken mixture on each tortilla; roll up, and place side by side, seam side down, in flat baking dish. Pour on remaining chili sauce. Sprinkle with remaining 1½ cups of cheese. Bake 20 to 30 minutes, or until heated through and cheese is melted and bubbly. Serve garnished with sour cream mixed with scallions or green onions and tops.   *6 servings*

Avocados Town Mein

---

3 firm avocados
1 lemon, cut in half
1 17-ounce package frozen chicken chow mein, partially
    thawed
2 tablespoons imitation bacon bits

&» Preheat oven to 325° F. Cut avocados in half
lengthwise, remove pits, and sprinkle with lemon juice to
prevent darkening. Fill each half with chow mein. Place
in shallow baking pan. Bake 20 minutes, or until completely warmed through. Sprinkle with bacon bits. Serve
hot (2 halves per person).

3 servings

CHICKEN BREASTS SUMATRA

---

3 chicken breasts, boned, skinned, and cut in half
Flour
4 tablespoons cooking oil or margarine
1 8-ounce package chicken flavor rice-and-vermicelli mix
½ cup chopped celery
¼ cup golden seedless raisins
¼ cup chopped cashew nuts

කෲ Preheat oven to 400° F. Dip chicken breasts in flour. In large ovenproof skillet with cover, sauté chicken in oil until golden (about 5 minutes each side). Remove from pan; keep warm. In same skillet, brown rice-vermicelli mixture, following directions on package. Add celery and raisins. Arrange chicken on top of rice mixture. Cover. Bake 45 minutes. Sprinkle with nuts just before serving.

6 servings

Chicken Quiescent

---

1 7-ounce package (*2 cups*) frozen cooked and diced
   chicken
1 10½-ounce can condensed cream of celery soup
1 3-ounce can broiled-in-butter mushrooms
1⅓ cups precooked minute-type rice, uncooked
2 tablespoons orange liqueur or 1 tablespoon frozen
   orange juice concentrate
1⅓ cups water
Instant parsley flakes (*optional*)

ᘒ Preheat oven to 375° F. Butter 1½-quart casserole.
In bowl, combine and mix all ingredients. Spoon into prepared casserole. Bake 30 minutes. Sprinkle with parsley
flakes for garnish.

4 to 6 servings

GREEN SALAD WITH GROUND BEEF DRESSING

1½ pounds ground beef
 1 envelope onion soup mix
 1 cup water
Few drops hot pepper sauce
 1 large head iceberg lettuce, torn into bite-size pieces
 2 medium tomatoes, cut into wedges
 ½ cup sliced green onions and tops
 ½ cup chopped green pepper
 ½ cup sliced ripe olives
 1 4-ounce package (*1 cup*) shredded Cheddar cheese
 1 6-ounce package corn chips, crushed

ॐ҇ In skillet, over high heat, quickly brown beef, chopping it into small granules as it cooks. Sprinkle soup mix over meat; add water and hot pepper sauce. Cover, reduce heat, and simmer 10 minutes. Remove cover; simmer 3 to 4 minutes more, or until liquid is reduced and mixture is not runny. Meanwhile, place lettuce pieces in salad bowl. Add tomatoes, onions, green pepper, olives, and cheese; toss lightly but well. Place salad mixture on 6 individual plates. Spoon hot meat sauce on top. Sprinkle with corn chips.   *6 servings*

HAM ALOHA WITH PEACHES

¾ cup chopped green pepper
¾ cup chopped celery
2 tablespoons margarine or cooking oil
1 10½-ounce can condensed cream of celery soup
1 1-pound 6-ounce can instant peach, apricot, or pineapple filling for pies
¼ cup water
2 tablespoons soy sauce
2½ cups cooked cubed ham
1 5-ounce can chow mein noodles or hot cooked instant rice
Shredded coconut

ও In large skillet, over medium-high heat, quickly sauté green pepper and celery in margarine or oil, until half cooked and still crisp. (Do not allow to become limp.) Stir in soup, pie filling, water, and soy sauce. Add ham. Cook just to boiling over medium heat, stirring to blend flavors. Serve over chow mein noodles or hot rice. Sprinkle lightly with coconut.

6 servings

CURRIED LOBSTER SALAD IN CANTALOUPE HALVES

---

2 medium cantaloupes, cut in half and seeded*
4 frozen (*1½ cups*) rock lobster tails, cooked, shelled, and cubed
1 8¾-ounce can (*1 cup*) pineapple tidbits
½ cup mayonnaise
2 tablespoons bottled creamy French dressing
2 tablespoons chopped bottled chutney
½ teaspoon curry powder
¼ cup chopped pecans
½ cup chopped celery

৯ Refrigerate cantaloupes and lobster while making dressing. Drain pineapple; reserve juice. In small bowl, combine mayonnaise, 2 tablespoons reserved pineapple juice, French dressing, chutney, and curry powder; blend well. In medium-sized bowl, combine lobster, pineapple tidbits, pecans, and celery; pour on dressing, and toss gently. Spoon into cantaloupe halves.

4 servings

* Use sharp knife to give pretty sawtooth edge to cantaloupe halves.

Louisiana Shrimp Salad

1⅓ cups precooked minute-type rice, uncooked
1 5- or 6½-ounce can (*1 cup*) shrimp, rinsed
¼ cup chopped green pepper
¾ cup diced fresh cauliflower
1 tablespoon minced green onion
1 tablespoon chopped ripe olives
¾ teaspoon salt or seasoning salt
⅓ cup mayonnaise
2 tablespoons lemon juice
2 tablespoons bottled creamy French dressing

᠘᠊ Preheat oven to 350° F. Prepare rice according to directions on package. Combine shrimp, green pepper, cauliflower, onion, olives, and salt; add to rice, and mix. In cup, combine mayonnaise, lemon juice, and French dressing; add to shrimp mixture, and toss lightly. To serve hot, bake about 20 minutes; or chill and serve cold on beds of lettuce leaves.

6 servings

BRIDGE PARTY CHICKEN SALAD

---

1 8-ounce package cream cheese, softened
1 cup commercial sour cream
½ teaspoon salt or seasoning salt
¼ teaspoon crumbled marjoram
1½ cups chopped celery
1 cup broken or chopped walnuts
¼ cup chopped green pepper
1½ 7-ounce packages (3 *cups*) frozen cooked and diced
   chicken
1 cup seedless grapes
1 1-pound 4-ounce can (2½ *cups*) pineapple tidbits or
   pineapple chunks
1 1-pound can (2 *cups*) jellied cranberry sauce, chilled

ᨐ In mixing bowl, beat together cream cheese, sour cream, salt, and marjoram. Stir in celery, nuts, and green pepper. Fold in chicken, grapes, and pineapple. Toss lightly to mix; chill until serving time. When serving, cut cranberry sauce into cubes or matchstick-style slices; arrange on top of chicken salad.

8 servings

Neptune Salad Bowl

---

1 9-ounce package frozen artichoke hearts
2 tablespoons butter
¼ teaspoon salt
¼ teaspoon garlic salt
½ cup chopped walnuts
1 medium cucumber, diced
1 tablespoon dried dill weed
½ teaspoon salt or seasoning salt
½ cup bottled French dressing
2 fresh unpeeled nectarines, cut into thin slices
1 4- to 5-ounce can (*1 cup*) medium deveined shrimp, rinsed and drained
1 4- to 5-ounce can (*1 cup*) lobster or crab meat, drained, picked over and flaked

ð➤ Cook artichoke hearts, following directions on package; drain. Melt butter in small skillet. Add salt, garlic salt, and walnuts, and sauté over medium heat, stirring constantly, until walnuts are buttery-browned and heated through. In salad bowl, combine artichoke hearts and remaining ingredients. Add walnuts to salad. Toss gently, but well.

6 servings

Albuquerque Salad

---

1 7¾-ounce can frozen avocado dip, thawed
⅓ cup commercial sour cream
2 tablespoons bottled Italian-style dressing
1 teaspoon instant minced onion
¾ teaspoon chili powder
¼ teaspoon salt
Dash of freshly ground pepper
2 cups shredded lettuce
1 1-pound can kidney beans, drained
2 medium tomatoes, chopped
1 tablespoon chopped green chilies
1 4½-ounce can (½ *cup*) chopped ripe olives
½ 4-ounce package (½ *cup*) shredded Cheddar cheese
½ cup coarsely crushed corn chips
1 hard-cooked egg, peeled and sliced
Paprika

ȝ✷ In small bowl, combine and mix avocado dip, sour cream, Italian dressing, onion, chili powder, salt, and pepper; set aside. In salad bowl, combine lettuce, beans, tomatoes, chilies, and olives; add avocado dressing and mix well. Arrange cheese and corn chips on top of salad; garnish with egg slices, and sprinkle with paprika.

4 to 6 servings

VEGETABLE ENSEMBLE NETTLETON

---

1 10-ounce package frozen French-style green beans
1 10-ounce package frozen peas
1 10-ounce package frozen baby lima beans
1 cup mayonnaise
2 hard-cooked eggs, peeled and chopped
3 tablespoons lemon juice
1 teaspoon instant minced onion
1 teaspoon Worcestershire sauce
1 teaspoon prepared mustard
¼ teaspoon garlic salt
1 to 2 teaspoons bacon-onion dip mix or bacon salad
    dressing mix (*shake package before opening*)

ᓚᕠ Butter 2½-quart casserole or serving dish. Cook
vegetables, following directions on package; drain. As
vegetables cook, combine remaining ingredients in saucepan; heat and stir until mixture comes just to boil. Remove from heat. Place vegetables in prepared dish. Pour
sauce over vegetables; stir to mix. Place vegetable en-
semble in oven at 350° F. for 10 minutes, or serve as is.

8 to 10 servings

Hawaiian Coconut Custard

---

1 6½- or 7½-ounce package vanilla or caramel frosting
   mix
½ cup hot water
⅔ cup commercial sour cream
3 eggs
¼ to ½ cup flaked coconut
½ teaspoon ground allspice

ह‣ Preheat oven to 350° F. In medium-sized bowl, combine frosting mix with water; stir well. Add sour cream, eggs, and coconut. Beat with beater or wire whisk until well blended. Pour into ovenproof custard cups or 1-quart baking dish. Sprinkle with allspice. Place in shallow pan on oven rack. Pour boiling water into pan to depth of 1 inch. Bake for 30 minutes for cups; 35 to 40 minutes for large baking dish. *4 to 5 servings*

Peach Nests

---

1 2⅛-ounce package whipped topping mix
1 teaspoon instant grated orange peel
⅓ cup chopped pecans or walnuts
2 12-ounce packages frozen sliced peaches, thawed but
   not soft
Melon balls (*optional*)

ह‣ Prepare whipped topping, following directions on package, but adding orange peel. Fold in nuts. Drop mixture by tablespoonful onto waxed paper. Use back of spoon to make round indentation on top of each nest.

Freeze until firm (about 2 to 3 hours). When ready to serve, spoon peaches into shells. Top with melon balls.

8 servings

SCANDINAVIAN PEACH MELBA

---

1 10-ounce package frozen red raspberries in instant-thaw
    pouch
6 canned, fresh, or frozen and thawed peeled peach halves
2 tablespoons rum (*optional*)
1 pint non-dairy whipped topping

ຽ❧ Follow directions on package for quick-thawing raspberries. Meanwhile, place each peach half in sherbet glass or dessert dish. Stir rum into whipped topping. Spoon flavored topping on peaches. Spoon on thawed berries. Serve immediately.

6 servings

CHERRY-CHOCOLATE PARFAITS

---

1 cup milk
1 cup commercial sour cream
½ teaspoon almond extract or 3 tablespoons light rum
1 3¾-ounce package instant vanilla pudding mix
1 1-pound 5-ounce can instant cherry filling for pies
    (*shake can before using*)
½ cup chopped nuts
Shaved chocolate

ຽ❧ In medium-sized mixing bowl, beat together milk, sour cream, and almond extract or rum. Add pudding mix;

beat thoroughly until blended. Fill parfait or dessert glasses or custard cups with alternate layers of pudding mixture, cherry pie filling, and nuts, ending with a dab of pudding mixture. Sprinkle with chocolate. Serve chilled.　　　　　　　　　　　　　　　*6 servings*

Mousse Grand Marnier

---

1 quart vanilla or French vanilla ice cream, slightly softened
¼ teaspoon instant grated orange peel
2 tablespoons Grand Marnier liqueur
Maraschino cherries with stems, or candied violets

Ɛᴥ Line muffin pan cups with paper liners (unless individual molds are used); set aside. In medium-sized bowl, combine ice cream, orange peel, and liqueur. With wooden spoon, lightly stir to blend flavors completely. Do not allow to melt. Spoon into individual paper bake cups or molds. Cover tightly with heavy aluminum foil so liqueur will not evaporate. Place in freezer 30 minutes, or until ready to serve. When serving decorate each with cherry or candied violet. (These freeze successfully up to a week or 10 days.)

8 servings

DESSERT DIVINITY

---

1 7-ounce jar marshmallow creme or 16 large marshmallows
1 pint non-dairy whipped topping
2 to 3 tablespoons Kahlua, Cointreau, Galliano, or Grand Marnier liqueur or 1 teaspoon vanilla extract
1 1-pound can Bartlett pear halves, drained

ॐ In top of double boiler over simmering water, melt marshmallow creme or marshmallows with ⅓ of topping, stirring constantly. When melted and smooth, stir in liqueur or vanilla. Cool. Blend the remaining whipped topping into cooled marshmallow mixture. Spoon into sherbet or parfait glasses, or pour into buttered mold. Refrigerate until serving time; or cover, and place in freezer until needed. (This freezes beautifully up to a week.) Top each serving with pear half.

4 to 6 servings

Russian Holiday Tea Czarina

---

5 cups water
¼ cup instant tea powder
¼ cup sugar
¼ cup orange-flavored breakfast drink powder
¼ cup frozen lemonade concentrate
6 whole cloves
½ stick cinnamon

ह Bring water to boil in medium-sized saucepan. (Meanwhile, run hot tap water into a 6-cup teapot to heat it.) To boiling water in saucepan, add remaining ingredients; stir. Remove from heat. Cover. Let stand 5 minutes to release and blend flavors. Empty water from warmed teapot; remove cloves and cinnamon stick from tea and pour tea into pot. Serve immediately. Tea may also be chilled and served over ice cubes.

6 servings

TROPICAL COOLER

---

1 tablespoon instant tea powder
3 tablespoons sugar
1¾ cups water
1 12-ounce can apricot or peach nectar
1 6-ounce can frozen lemonade concentrate
2 12-ounce bottles lemon-lime carbonated beverage

ह≫ In pitcher or mixing bowl, dissolve tea and sugar in water. Add fruit nectar and lemonade concentrate; stir. Pour ½ to ¾ cup mixture into each tall glass; fill with ice cubes, then add carbonated beverage to top of glass, and stir. Garnish with colored straw.

6 to 8 servings

ICED TEA SWIZZLE

---

4 cups instant or brewed tea
2 tablespoons frozen lemonade concentrate
2 tablespoons frozen limeade concentrate
1 cup cranberry juice
1 12-ounce can or bottle ginger ale

ह≫ Tea need not be hot. Combine all ingredients in pitcher; stir. Serve over ice cubes in tall glasses.

6 servings

Dinner

BE BRIGHT AND JOVIAL

AMONG YOUR GUESTS TONIGHT

—Shakespeare

Wine Marinated Brussels Sprouts

---

1 10-ounce package frozen baby Brussels sprouts
½ teaspoon seasoned pepper
½ teaspoon salt
½ teaspoon dill seed
⅓ cup bottled Italian-style dressing
2 tablespoons red wine

ৡ Prepare Brussels sprouts, following directions on package, but adding pepper, salt, and dill seed. Cook *just until crunchy;* do *not* allow them to boil. (Sprouts will become mushy if overcooked.) Drain. Put in bowl with cover. Add dressing and wine; stir gently to cover all sprouts with marinade. Cover. Let stand at room temperature 1 hour. Refrigerate until ready to serve, or if you are short on time, place in freezer for about 30 minutes. Serve with toothpicks as an appetizer, or as a salad.

6 appetizer servings
or 3 salad servings

Viennese Cocktail Cookies
(Puff Pastry Hors d'oeuvre)

---

1 10-ounce package frozen unbaked patty shells, thawed
　　but *not* warm
¾ cup grated Parmesan cheese
1 egg beaten with 1 extra egg yolk

ౘ⋟ Preheat oven to 450° F. Remove patty shells from
wrapping. Sprinkle breadboard with ¼ cup grated Parmesan cheese. Place patty shells, sides touching, on cheese
and roll them out to form dough ⅛-inch thick. With
cookie cutter or knife, cut out cookies in shape to suit
your fancy. Brush top side of each cookie with beaten
egg; dredge egg-painted side in remaining ½ cup cheese,
and place, dredged side up, on ungreased cookie sheet.
Bake 3 minutes; *reduce* heat to 300° F. and bake until dark
golden brown (about 7 minutes). Serve cookies for cocktail bites; or put 2 cookies together with a cream cheese
spread (sandwich-style); or top each with a dollop of
sour cream and caviar.

About 2 dozen

HOT PATE HORS D'OEUVRE

---

1 8-ounce package refrigerated quick crescent dinner rolls
2 4¾-ounce cans liverwurst spread
¼ cup imitation bacon bits
¼ cup minced or thinly sliced green onion
Seasoning salt

&~ Preheat oven to 350° F. Remove roll dough from package; separate at perforations. Generously spread liverwurst over dough; then cut each triangle of dough into 4 triangles. Sprinkle bacon bits, onion, and salt to taste over liverwurst, and use fingers or broad knife to pat in lightly. Fold tip of triangle over wide part to make a little roll. Place on ungreased cookie sheet. Bake 12 minutes, or until golden. Serve hot.   *32 appetizers*

LOVE-AT-FIRST-BITE PARTY DIP

---

1 7¾-ounce can frozen avocado dip, thawed
1 cup cream-style cottage cheese
½ cup commercial sour cream
1 teaspoon lemon juice
1 2¼-ounce can deviled ham
1 teaspoon grated onion (*optional*)

&~ In blender or mixing bowl, blend all ingredients until almost smooth. Serve chilled dip with vegetable dippers such as celery, carrot, and cucumber sticks, radish roses, cherry tomatoes, and cauliflowerettes. Or serve with corn chips and assorted crackers.   *2½ cups*

HOT SEAFOOD PINWHEELS

Filling

1 6½-ounce can crab meat, drained and flaked
1 4½-ounce can shrimp, drained and chopped
¼ cup minced celery
¼ cup mayonnaise
1 tablespoon chopped parsley

ટ≫ Combine all ingredients in medium-sized bowl; mix well and set aside.

Dough

1 packaged pie crust stick or ½ 9- to 11-ounce package pie crust mix
½ teaspoon prepared mustard
2 tablespoons boiling clam-tomato or tomato juice
Ketchup

ટ≫ Preheat oven to 400° F. Grease cookie sheet. Prepare pastry, following directions on package for 1 pie crust, but adding mustard and using juice instead of water. On floured breadboard, roll out dough to 15 × 6-inch rectangle. Spread with filling. Roll up jelly-roll style. Cut into ½-inch slices. Place on prepared cookie sheet. Bake 10 to 12 minutes, or until golden. Serve with warmed ketchup.   *24 appetizers*
or 6 dinner servings

HAM BOATS

---

12 4-inch square slices cooked ham
1 cup mayonnaise or hollandaise sauce
3 to 4 teaspoons dry cheese-flavored salad seasoning mix
1 10½-ounce can asparagus tips, drained

ᔆ Preheat broiler. Lay ham slices out on breadboard or counter. In small bowl, combine and mix together mayonnaise or hollandaise sauce and seasoning mix. Spread ¾ of mayonnaise mixture equally over slices of ham. Place 1 asparagus spear on each ham slice, and roll up jelly-roll style. Spread tops of rolls with remaining ¼ mayonnaise mixture. Cut each roll into 3 bite-size pieces. Place on ungreased cookie sheet. Broil until heated through and bubbly. Serve warm using toothpicks for spears.

About 3 dozen appetizers

December Dip
(*Shrimp and Pimiento Dip*)

1 10-ounce can frozen condensed cream of shrimp soup
1 8-ounce package cream cheese
1 tablespoon instant parsley flakes
3 tablespoons finely chopped pimiento
½ teaspoon Worcestershire sauce
1 teaspoon chili powder
1 tablespoon sherry

჻ Allow soup to thaw in pan of hot water for 30 minutes unopened; meanwhile, unwrap cream cheese and allow it to soften at room temperature. In medium-sized bowl, combine and beat all ingredients until not quite smooth. Do not over-beat, as dip will become watery. Serve chilled with chips for a dip, or with crackers for a spread. Use any leftover dip as a sauce for hot cooked cauliflower. *2½ cups*

Pizza Kabobs

---

1 6-ounce package frozen party-size pizza rolls; slightly thawed
1 green pepper, seeded and cut into 12 1-inch pieces
12 medium mushrooms, wiped clean with damp cloth
12 canned pineapple chunks
Salad oil

჻ If using wooden or bamboo skewers, plunge in water to moisten first, to prevent scorching. Thread each skewer with 1 pizza roll, green pepper slice, mushroom, and pineapple chunk. Brush vegetables lightly with oil. Broil 8 inches from source of heat, turning once, until heated through. Serve immediately. These are good cooked over glowing charcoal, as well. *12 appetizers*

SAVORY FRANKS CROUSTADINE

4 tablespoons butter or margarine, softened
2 teaspoons prepared mustard
1 8-ounce package refrigerated quick crescent dinner rolls
24 cocktail frankfurters
2 tablespoons sesame seed (*optional*)

ও Preheat oven to 375° F. Grease cookie sheet. In small bowl, use fork to mash together 2 tablespoons butter or margarine and mustard. Unroll dough; separate it into 4 rectangular pieces. (Press diagonal perforation of each triangle with fingertips to close little holes.) Spread rectangles with butter mixture. Cut each rectangle into 6 strips crosswise, making 24 strips in all. Place frankfurter at end of each strip, then roll dough around it, pinching the end closed with fingertips. Place on prepared sheet. Brush with remaining 2 tablespoons butter or margarine. Sprinkle with sesame seeds, pressing seeds into dough. Bake 10 minutes, or until golden.

24 appetizers

American Vichyssoise

---

2 teaspoons granules or 2 cubes instant chicken bouillon
2 cups boiling water
1 cup cream
1 cup instant mashed potato flakes
1 3-ounce package cream cheese with chives
¼ teaspoon salt
½ cup seedless white grapes or diced cucumber or tomato

ঌ In small bowl, dissolve bouillon in boiling water. Add cream; stir in potato flakes. Pour into blender or mixing bowl. Add cream cheese and salt; beat or blend until smooth. Chill. Serve garnished with grapes, cucumber, or tomato (or a combination of these).

4 servings

Yogurt Soup Budapest

---

1 teaspoon granules or 1 cube instant chicken bouillon
1 cup boiling water
½ cup seedless raisins
1 medium cucumber, peeled and cut into ½-inch slices
3 cups plain yogurt
½ teaspoon salt or seasoning salt
⅛ teaspoon white pepper
2 tablespoons freeze-dried chives
½ teaspoon dill weed

ह॒ॐ In small bowl, dissolve bouillon in boiling water;
add raisins and set aside. In blender or mixing bowl, combine cucumber, yogurt, salt, pepper, chives, and dill;
blend or beat until smooth. Add bouillon and raisins.
Blend or beat until almost smooth. Serve chilled.

6 servings

Halibut Florentine

---

2 10-ounce packages frozen chopped spinach
1 tablespoon instant minced onion
2 tablespoons olive oil
2 tablespoons wine vinegar
6 (*2 pounds*) frozen halibut steaks, thawed
¼ cup (*½ stick*) butter, softened
Seasoning salt
Paprika

ट&❧ Preheat oven to 350° F. Butter large flat baking dish. In saucepan, cook spinach with onion, following directions on package. Drain. Sprinkle with oil and vinegar; toss to blend flavors. Place halibut in prepared dish. Spoon hot spinach over halibut, arranging it nicely on each steak. Dot with butter; sprinkle with salt and paprika. Bake 15 to 20 minutes, or until fish flakes easily at the point of a knife.   *6 servings*

Baked Halibut Macadamia

---

6 (*2 pounds*) frozen halibut steaks, thawed
Butter or margarine
Shrimp-Macadamia Sauce (*below*)

ટ≈ Preheat oven to 450° F. Generously butter large flat
baking dish. Place halibut in prepared dish; dot generously with butter or margarine. Pour Shrimp-Macadamia
Sauce over fish. Bake 20 to 30 minutes, or until fish flakes
easily at the point of a knife. Do not baste or turn.

6 servings

Shrimp-Macadamia Sauce

---

1 10-ounce can frozen condensed cream of shrimp soup,
    thawed
2 teaspoons bottled chili sauce
½ cup salted chopped macadamia nuts
½ teaspoon salt
⅛ teaspoon pepper

ટ≈ Combine all ingredients in small saucepan. Stir and
heat slowly just to boiling. Serve warm over cooked
halibut, perch, sole, flounder, pike, or omelets.   *2 cups*

Elegantly Sauced Halibut

---

  2 1-pound packages frozen halibut or salmon steaks
  ¼ cup (½ *stick*) butter
1½ cups chopped tomatoes
  ½ cup chopped onion
  1 teaspoon salt
  ½ teaspoon paprika
  ½ teaspoon crumbled sweet basil
  ¼ teaspoon freshly ground pepper
  ⅓ cup water or sherry
  1 1⅛-ounce package hollandaise sauce mix

ફ• Partially thaw halibut or salmon steaks; then cut into serving-size pieces. Melt butter in medium saucepan. Add tomatoes, onion, salt, paprika, sweet basil, and pepper; bring to boil. Stir in water or sherry and hollandaise mix; stir until smooth. Allow mixture to return to boil; simmer 1 minute. Place fish steaks in large flat baking dish; pour on sauce. Cover with aluminum foil. Bake at 425° F. for 25 to 30 minutes, or until fish flakes easily at the point of a knife.

6 servings

BROILED SALMON WITH
SAUCE BEARNAISE

---

2 1-pound packages frozen salmon or halibut steaks
Butter
Salt
Pepper
1 1⅛-ounce package hollandaise sauce mix
½ teaspoon instant grated lemon peel
2 tablespoons lemon juice
1 teaspoon instant minced onion
1 teaspoon instant parsley flakes
1 tablespoon tarragon vinegar
1 tablespoon white wine

 Partially thaw salmon or halibut steaks; then cut into serving-size pieces. Preheat broiler. Butter bottom of broiler pan. Place fish steaks in pan. Dot with butter; sprinkle with salt and pepper to taste. Broil 4 inches from heat for 5 to 6 minutes per side, or until fish flakes easily at the point of a knife. As fish broils, make hollandaise sauce, following directions on package, but using only ½ cup water called for and stirring in remaining ingredients. Serve sauce over broiled fish steaks.

6 servings

FILLET OF SOLE FANTASIE

---

2 1-pound packages frozen sole fillets, thawed
1 cup commercial sour cream
1 envelope mushroom soup mix
1/16 teaspoon *each* powdered thyme and oregano
¼ teaspoon *each* crumbled sweet basil and marjoram
2 tablespoons white wine
1 tablespoon lemon juice
2 tablespoons freeze-dried chives
2 tablespoons grated Parmesan cheese

ৡ Preheat oven to 350° F. Butter large flat baking dish. Arrange fillets in prepared dish. In small bowl, combine and mix sour cream, soup mix, thyme, oregano, sweet basil, marjoram, wine, and lemon juice. Spoon over fish. Bake 20 to 25 minutes, or until fish flakes easily at the point of a knife. Remove from oven. Sprinkle with chives and cheese; brown under broiler.

6 servings

Mahimahi in Sweet and Sour Sauce

---

2 1-pound packages frozen fillets (*mahimahi, sole, or perch*)
1 cup packaged biscuit mix
½ cup milk
½ cup chopped almonds
Butter or margarine
Sweet and Sour Sauce (*below*)
Sesame seeds (*optional*)

ે❧ Thaw fillets enough to separate; then cut into serving-size pieces. In pie plate, combine and mix biscuit mix and milk. Dip fillets in batter and pat on almonds. Melt butter or margarine in skillet. Sauté fillets, skin side up, until brown and almost crisp on one side. Turn, brown other side until fish flakes easily with the point of a knife. Serve with Sweet and Sour Sauce. Sprinkle lightly with sesame seeds.   *6 servings*

Sweet and Sour Sauce

---

1 6-ounce can frozen orange juice concentrate, thawed
¼ cup prepared mustard
¼ cup brown sugar, firmly packed
1 tablespoon soy sauce
1 tablespoon dry sherry (*optional*)
½ teaspoon ginger powder

ે❧ In blender or mixing bowl, combine and blend juice concentrate, mustard, and sugar. Add soy sauce, sherry, and ginger; blend. Heat through and serve over cooked fish or brush on fish during cooking.   *1½ cups*

PAELLA VALENCIA

---

1   24-ounce package frozen rock lobster tails
1   32-ounce package frozen cooked and breaded chicken
      pieces (*10 pieces*)
¼   cup olive or salad oil
1¾   cups converted rice
2   cloves garlic, minced
½   teaspoon saffron powder
2   14-ounce cans chicken broth
1   teaspoon instant minced onion
1   tomato, cut into 8 wedges
½   pound frozen peeled and deveined shrimp
1   2-ounce jar sliced pimientos
1   10-ounce package frozen peas

ↄ❧ Partially thaw lobster tails and chicken. Preheat oven to 350° F. Heat oil in large Dutch oven; sauté rice and garlic until delicately browned, adding more oil if needed. Add saffron powder, broth, and onion. Cover; cook over medium heat 10 minutes. Meanwhile, remove thin under-shell of lobster tails with scissors; bend back shells to make tails lie flat. Arrange chicken pieces, lobster tails, tomato wedges, and shrimp on rice; cover, and bake 25 minutes. Add pimiento and peas, stir carefully, and bake 15 minutes more. Serve directly from cooking pan.   *6 servings*

Nasi Goreng
(Indonesian Fried Rice)

½ cup (*1 stick*) butter
1 medium onion, chopped
1 medium green pepper, seeded and chopped
1 6-ounce package curried rice mix
2 teaspoons chicken bouillon granules
2½ cups water
1½ pounds peeled, deveined, cooked shrimp, cut in half
½ cup cooked diced chicken
½ cup cooked diced ham
½ cup cooked flaked crab meat

ह‍~ Melt butter in large heavy skillet or Dutch oven. Add onion, green pepper, and packet of rice from mix. Sauté over medium heat 5 minutes, or until rice is golden. Add bouillon granules and packet of seasoning from rice mix. Simmer 2 to 3 minutes, but do not allow seasoning to scorch. Add water, shrimp, chicken, and ham. Cover; cook 25 minutes, or until rice is cooked and all liquid is absorbed. Serve garnished with crab meat flakes. (Or if you feel ambitious, top each serving with a sunny-side up fried egg.)   *6 servings*

Birds of Paradise
(Chicken Breasts in Cherry Jubilee Sauce)

---

3 chicken breasts, boned, skinned, and cut in half
¼ cup flour
½ teaspoon salt
⅛ teaspoon white pepper
2 tablespoons butter or margarine
1 1-pound can dark pitted sweet cherries
2 tablespoons kirsch
1 envelope chicken rice soup mix
1 cup boiling water
⅓ cup dry white wine or chicken broth

 Wipe chicken breasts with damp cloth or paper towel. Combine flour, salt, and pepper. Dust chicken breasts with seasoned flour. Melt butter in large skillet. Quickly sauté chicken, turning to brown all sides. Meanwhile, drain cherries, reserving juice, and place in small bowl. Sprinkle cherries with kirsch. In separate bowl, combine soup mix, water, and juice from cherries. Stir to blend flavors, then add to sautéed chicken breasts. Cover; cook over low heat 20 minutes, or until tender. Remove breasts to heated platter; keep warm. Add wine or broth to pan liquids and cook over high heat, stirring, until liquid thickens. Add cherries and kirsch; heat through. Serve cherry sauce over chicken breasts. *6 servings*

JAPANESE SHISH KEBAB OR GRILLED BIRD

---

6 broiler-fryer chicken thighs
3 broiler-fryer chicken breasts
1 envelope instant meat marinade
¼ cup soy sauce
¼ cup dry sherry
¼ cup water
¼ cup peanut, sesame, or corn oil
1 green pepper, seeded and cut into 6 chunks
6 scallions

ৡ Have butcher skin chicken and cut meat off bones into 1-inch pieces. (You can use the bones for stock later.) In large shallow baking dish or pan, combine marinade, soy sauce, sherry, and water. Mix to smooth consistency, using wire whisk. Thread chicken pieces on 6 metal or bamboo skewers, alternating pieces of thigh and breast. Gently dip and swish each skewer in marinade. Dip chunk of green pepper and scallion into marinade and add to end of each skewer. Broil over glowing gray charcoal, or under preheated broiler, brushing with leftover marinade several times during cooking. Turn skewers over once to cook each side evenly. Do not overcook, or chicken will dry out (about 4 to 5 minutes on each side). *6 servings*

GAME HEN IN LEMON SAUCE

3 Cornish game hens, split in half
1 6-ounce can frozen lemonade concentrate, thawed
1 cup ketchup
½ cup water
¼ cup white wine
2 tablespoons Worcestershire sauce
¼ cup prepared mustard
¼ cup (½ *stick*) butter
2 tablespoons instant minced onion

ટ❧ Wash game hens and pat dry. In small saucepan, combine lemonade concentrate, ketchup, water, and wine; stir until smooth. Add Worcestershire sauce, mustard, butter, and onion. Bring mixture to boil over medium-high heat; reduce heat, and cover. Simmer 10 minutes, stirring frequently, to allow flavors to mellow together. Broil hen halves, skin side down, for 12 minutes, brushing frequently with sauce. Turn; brush with sauce, and broil 12 minutes more, brushing frequently with sauce, until golden brown and tender. Or cook over glowing charcoal, brushing frequently, until done as desired. Serve any remaining sauce with hens.　　　　　　　　　　*6 servings*

Baked Chicken Breasts Versailles

---

3 chicken breasts, boned, skinned, and cut in half
6 thin slices (*4 × 4-inch*) cooked ham
6 thin slices (*4 × 4-inch*) Swiss cheese
¼ cup chicken broth or white wine
1 2⅜-ounce package seasoned coating mix for chicken
6 slices canned pimiento

ટે Preheat oven to 400° F. Have unbuttered flat baking dish ready. On breadboard, between 2 sheets of waxed paper, pound each chicken breast ½- to ⅛-inch thick. On each breast place slice of ham and cheese; roll up jelly-roll style and skewer closed with toothpick. Brush with broth or wine, and dip in coating mix, coating all exposed sides as evenly as possible. Place on baking dish. Bake 20 minutes, or until golden and tender. Garnish with pimiento. If calories are of no concern, serve with Velvet Sauce.   *6 servings*

Velvet Sauce

---

1 cup commercial sour cream
1 10½-ounce can condensed cream of mushroom soup
⅓ cup dry vermouth (*optional*)

ટે In small saucepan, combine and heat sour cream and soup.   *2½ cups*

Chuck Steak Picado

2 teaspoons non-seasoned meat tenderizer
1 3½- to 4-pound choice or prime boneless beef chuck
    steak
3 tablespoons onion soup mix (*shake package before
    opening*)
2 tablespoons sugar
¼ teaspoon pepper or seasoned pepper
1 tablespoon prepared mustard
½ cup ketchup
¼ cup wine or cider vinegar
1 tablespoon lemon juice
⅛ teaspoon fennel
¾ cup water

⅔ Preheat broiler. Sprinkle tenderizer on meat, following directions on label. Place meat on rack of broiler pan. Broil 4 to 6 inches from heat 10 minutes on each side for medium-rare, or until done as desired. While meat broils, combine remaining ingredients in small saucepan. Bring mixture to boil; reduce heat. Cover, and simmer 10 minutes, stirring occasionally. When meat is broiled, cut across the grain into thin slices. Serve covered with sauce, or pass the sauce in gravy boat.

4 to 6 servings

Busy Day Pepper Steak

---

1 3-inch thick (*6 to 7 pounds*) bone-in sirloin
1 5-ounce bottle soy sauce
½ 2¹¹⁄₁₆-ounce bottle lemon pepper

 This meat must marinate for 3 days. Place steak in deep dish or pan. Sprinkle top liberally with soy sauce, using about one-sixth of the bottle, then sprinkle with lemon pepper as heavily. Cover with aluminum foil or lid; refrigerate. Turn twice daily, or more, recoating each time with soy sauce and lemon pepper. Keep tightly covered between turnings. If you use up all the soy sauce and lemon pepper, continue to turn the meat to insure that it is moist in the pan marinade. To cook: preheat broiler or have glowing charcoal ready. Broil steak at least 3 inches from heat 25 to 30 minutes on each side for medium-rare, or until done to taste.

8 servings

Beef Wellington

---

1 4-pound fillet of beef (*at room temperature*)
3 tablespoons brandy
Salt
Freshly ground pepper
6 slices bacon
1 1¾-ounce can chicken liver paté
1 10-ounce package frozen unbaked patty shells, thawed
    but *not* warm
1 egg, beaten

꒱ Preheat oven to 350° F. Place fillet on rack in shallow roasting pan; brush well with brandy on all sides. Sprinkle with salt and pepper to taste. Cover with bacon slices. Roast 40 minutes (rare). Remove from oven; cool. Increase oven heat to 425° F. Spread cooled beef with liver paté. Remove package wrapping from patty shells. On breadboard press 6 patty shells together; roll out as thin as possible. Wrap beef in pastry, trimming and tucking the edges, but not making pastry double thick anywhere except side and middle seams. Brush pastry top with beaten egg. Prick with fork, or cut designs or diagonal slits to allow steam to escape during cooking. Place in center rack of oven. Bake until pastry is crisp, flaky, and golden (about 30 minutes), or until meat thermometer inserted in center of meat registers 130° F.

6 servings

ARMENIAN BEEF KABOBS

1½ pounds sirloin tip steak
1 6-ounce can tomato paste
⅔ cup bottled Italian-style dressing
¼ cup water
Few drops hot pepper sauce
1 tablespoon Worcestershire sauce
1 teaspoon celery seed
1 1-pound can whole small white onions, drained
2 green peppers, seeded and cut into 2-inch squares
Salad oil

ᖰ❧ Trim meat of all fat and gristle. Cut into 1½-inch cubes. In medium-sized bowl, combine and mix tomato paste, Italian dressing, water, hot pepper sauce, Worcestershire sauce, and celery seed. Place meat cubes in sauce, turning to coat all sides evenly. Marinate 45 minutes, turning frequently. Thread meat on skewers alternately with onions and green pepper squares. Brush vegetables lightly with salad oil. Broil 10 to 15 minutes, turning to brown all sides, and basting frequently with marinade during cooking. Kabobs may be cooked over glowing charcoal, too.   *6 servings*

Stir-fry Pepper Steak

1½ to 2 pounds top quality flank steak
4 tablespoons butter or margarine
1 envelope onion soup mix
2 cups water
½ teaspoon ginger powder
3 tablespoons soy sauce
4 teaspoons cornstarch
2 tablespoons sherry
2 green peppers, seeded and cut into strips

ಶಿ Cut steak into 3 equal pieces crosswise, then cut each piece lengthwise (with grain) into ⅛-inch thick strips. Melt butter or margarine in large skillet. Sauté meat strips until browned on all sides. Add soup mix, water, ginger, and soy sauce; stir. Cover; simmer 20 minutes. Mix cornstarch into sherry; stir into meat mixture. Cook 2 minutes. Add green pepper strips. Cook 5 minutes. Serve over hot fluffy rice.

6 servings

Something Special Meat Loaf

---

1 pound ground cooked ham
1 pound ground beef
2 cups packaged soup-and-salad croutons or plain stuffing
    mix
1 1-pound 6-ounce can instant apple filling for pies (*shake
    can before opening*)
2 eggs, slightly beaten
¼ cup wine (*optional*)
2 tablespoons chopped onion
1 tablespoon chopped green pepper
Freshly ground pepper

ছ Preheat oven to 350° F. In large bowl, combine ground meats, croutons or stuffing mix, 1 cup only of the pie filling, eggs, wine, onion, green pepper, and pepper to taste; toss lightly but well to mix. Pat into 8-inch square baking dish, or place on double thickness of heavy-duty aluminum foil and pat into round loaf shape. (If wrapping in foil, fold up sides, leaving a little air space above meat, and fold closed tightly.) Bake 30 to 40 minutes, or place aluminum covered loaf over glowing charcoal for 40 minutes. Remove from oven or charcoal fire, spread meat with remaining pie filling, bake or cook 15 minutes more. Spoon off excess meat juices before serving. *8 servings*

SALTIMBOCCA
(*Medallions of Ham and Veal*)

---

6 very thin slices of veal, each about 5 inches square
Freshly ground pepper
½ teaspoon dried sage
6 slices prosciutto ham
2 tablespoons butter
1 envelope dry Italian salad dressing mix
⅓ cup dry white wine

ৡ Have butcher pound veal slices very thin. Sprinkle each piece lightly with pepper and sage. (Do not use salt as the prosciutto is salty enough.) Cut the prosciutto the same size as the veal, and place 1 ham slice over each veal slice. Secure with toothpicks. Melt butter in skillet. Brown the meat, ham side first, for 2 minutes; turn and brown veal side for 5 minutes. Meanwhile, make salad dressing, following directions on package, but substituting wine for vinegar *and* water. Pour dressing over browned meat; cover, and continue cooking over low heat 5 minutes more, or until veal is tender. Remove toothpicks before serving.

6 servings

Veal Champagne

1½ pounds thin veal scallops
6 tablespoons butter
1 1¾-ounce package chicken gravy mix
¾ cup champagne or white Burgundy wine
Instant parsley flakes

ଌ Have butcher pound veal scallops very thin. Melt butter in large skillet. Sauté veal over medium heat until nicely browned on both sides. Meanwhile, in small saucepan, make gravy, following directions on package, but using half water and half champagne or wine. Remove meat to heated serving plate or platter. Spoon champagne sauce over meat. Sprinkle with parsley flakes.

6 servings

VEAL OSKAR

1½ pounds thin veal scallops
½ cup flour
1 egg, beaten with 2 tablespoons water or white wine
½ cup packaged bread crumbs
½ cup (*1 stick*) butter
2 10-ounce packages cut broccoli, frozen in cheese sauce
1 6½-ounce can (*1 cup*) crab meat, drained, picked over, and flaked
6 tablespoons mayonnaise
Paprika

ဒ☙ Have butcher pound veal scallops very thin. Dust with flour. Dip in beaten egg, then in crumbs. Melt butter in ovenproof skillet; cook meat in butter 2 to 4 minutes on each side, or until tender. Meanwhile cook broccoli, following directions on package. Place on each meat scallop a layer of cooked broccoli, flaked crab meat, and mayonnaise. Sprinkle with paprika. Place under broiler until crab meat is well heated through and top is bubbly (about 5 minutes).

6 servings

Pork Chops Figaro

---

6 center cut pork chops, cut ¾-inch thick
½ cup canned or instant beef gravy
1 1½-ounce package dry spaghetti sauce mix
1 teaspoon chili powder
¾ cup water
¼ cup packaged cornflake crumbs

కౖ Preheat oven to 375° F. Place chops on rack of broiler pan. Bake 10 minutes. Meanwhile, in small bowl, combine gravy, spaghetti sauce mix, chili powder, and water; stir until smooth. Remove chops from oven; cover with half of the sauce and sprinkle with half of the crumbs. Return to oven and bake 20 minutes. Remove chops from oven and cover with remaining half of the sauce and crumbs. Bake 15 minutes more, or until done.

6 servings

LIVER STROGANOFF
(*Liver and Mushrooms in Sour Cream*)

1½ pounds calves liver, cut into 1-inch cubes
3 tablespoons minced onion
3 tablespoons butter or margarine
2 4-ounce cans sliced mushrooms, drained
1½ cups beef consommé or instant beef bouillon
1 cup commercial sour cream
3 tablespoons flour
1 teaspoon salt
¼ teaspoon lemon pepper
Dash of nutmeg

ई In heavy skillet, quickly brown liver cubes and onion in melted butter or margarine. Reduce heat, and simmer 3 minutes. Add mushrooms; sauté 2 minutes more. In medium-sized bowl, combine and blend all remaining ingredients. Pour over liver. Heat through, but do not boil. Serve on toast or over hot buttered noodles or rice.

6 servings

Baked Fennel

---

2 heads fennel, trimmed (*reserve leaves*)
Boiling salted water
¼ cup (½ *stick*) butter or margarine
2 tablespoons packaged bread or cornflake crumbs
1 tablespoon grated Parmesan cheese
1 hard-cooked egg, peeled and chopped
1 teaspoon instant parsley flakes

ह≈ Cut heads of fennel lengthwise into fourths. Plunge into boiling water; boil just until tender (about 8 minutes); drain well. Meanwhile, finely chop 1 tablespoon reserved fennel leaves; set aside. Butter large flat baking dish. Arrange fennel fourths in dish. Dot with butter or margarine, then sprinkle with crumbs, cheese, chopped fennel leaves, egg, and parsley flakes. Bake at 400° F. until heated through and cheese is melted (about 10 minutes).

6 servings

Raspberry-Strawberry Holiday Mold

---

1 3-ounce package strawberry-flavored gelatin
1 3-ounce package raspberry-flavored gelatin
1½ cups boiling water
1 10-ounce package frozen red raspberries in instant-thaw pouch, thawed according to directions on package, and drained (*reserve juice*)
1 10-ounce package frozen strawberries in instant-thaw pouch, thawed according to directions on package, and drained (*reserve juice*)
Juice reserved from strawberries and raspberries, with enough water or rosé wine to make 1½ cups
1 8½- or 9-ounce can crushed pineapple with juice
1 cup commercial sour cream or 1 cup cream-style cottage cheese
1 tablespoon non-dairy creamer powder
½ cup chopped or broken pecans

ᔣ In saucepan or large bowl with pouring spout, dissolve gelatins in boiling water. Stir in raspberries, strawberries, reserved juices and water, and pineapple with juice. Pour half of gelatin mixture into 2-quart mold; refrigerate until set. (Do not refrigerate remaining half of gelatin.) In bowl, combine sour cream or cottage cheese, creamer powder, and pecans; stir to mix. Spread over molded gelatin. Spoon remaining half of gelatin over top; refrigerate until set. Unmold and serve on lettuce leaves.

8 to 10 servings

RAW MUSHROOM SALAD

---

1 **pound raw mushrooms**
¼ **cup olive or salad oil**
3 **tablespoons fresh lemon or lime juice**
1 **teaspoon bacon-onion, onion and horseradish, or green onion dip mix (*shake package before opening*)**
¼ **teaspoon lemon pepper**
½ **teaspoon salt**
2 **teaspoons prepared mustard**
1 **cup diced celery**
1 **hard-cooked egg, peeled and chopped**

ঠ✤ Quickly wash mushrooms and pat dry or wipe them with damp cloth. Slice mushrooms very thin. In salad bowl, combine all ingredients except egg. Toss lightly. Place salad mixture on 6 serving plates. Garnish each salad with chopped egg.

6 servings

LIMA BEANS A LA ROQUEFORT

2 10-ounce packages frozen baby lima beans
2 teaspoons granules or 2 cubes chicken bouillon
6 ounces (¾ *cup*) crumbled Roquefort or blue cheese
Bottled beef gravy and seasoning base
4 tablespoons packaged cornflake crumbs
Butter
Paprika

Preheat oven to 350° F. Cook lima beans, following directions on package; drain but reserve juice. Dissolve chicken bouillon granules or cubes in hot reserved juice; set aside. Arrange alternately layers of lima beans, cheese, few drops liquid gravy base, and a sprinkling of crumbs; repeat layer process. Pour chicken-flavored juice over casserole, dot heavily with butter, and sprinkle with paprika. Bake 15 minutes, or until bubbly and done.

6 servings

STIR-FRIED CABBAGE

½ cup (*1 stick*) butter or margarine
1 8-ounce package (*4 cups*) cole slaw mixture
1 teaspoon salt
¼ teaspoon seasoned pepper

ঽ In skillet or saucepan, heat butter or margarine *very* hot. Add cole slaw mixture; cook 8 to 10 minutes, tossing vigorously until almost tender. Mix in seasonings, stirring vigorously. Cover; cook 5 minutes more if you wish it more tender. Serve immediately.   *4 servings*

STIR-FRIED ASPARAGUS AND MUSHROOMS

---

2 10-ounce packages frozen asparagus spears, almost
     thawed
5 tablespoons cooking oil
1 4-ounce can mushroom stems and pieces, drained
1 teaspoon seasoning salt

ঽ Cut each asparagus spear lengthwise into 2 pieces, then cut each piece diagonally into two or three pieces.* In skillet or saucepan, heat oil *very* hot. Add asparagus; cook 4 to 6 minutes, tossing vigorously to fry all sides, until almost tender. Stir in mushrooms and salt; heat through, stirring continually. Serve immediately.

4 servings

* Cutting asparagus in this manner exposes the inner fiber and allows the vegetable to cook quickly and absorb all flavors.

ARTICHOKE HEARTS WITH SWISS CHEESE

---

2 9-ounce packages frozen artichoke hearts
1 4-ounce can mushroom stems and pieces, drained (*reserve juice*)
1 1¾-ounce package chicken gravy mix
¼ teaspoon dried rosemary
⅛ teaspoon crushed marjoram
1 tablespoon white wine
1 cup cubed Swiss cheese
1 cup packaged soup-and-salad croutons

ॐ In saucepan, cook artichoke hearts, following directions on package; drain. Butter 1½-quart flat baking dish. Arrange artichokes and mushrooms in prepared dish. In separate saucepan, prepare gravy, following directions on package, but using 1 cup water and reserved mushroom juice for liquid called for, and adding rosemary, marjoram, and wine. Cover artichokes and mushrooms with layers of cheese cubes, croutons, and then gravy. Bake at 350° F. for 20 minutes.

6 servings

CAULIFLOWER BLEUS FRANCAIS
(Cauliflower in Blue Cheese Sauce)

---

2 10-ounce packages frozen cauliflower
1 envelope dry blue cheese salad dressing mix
1 cup commercial sour cream
½ cup packaged soup-and-salad croutons
½ cup fresh chopped mushrooms

ह‍ৡ In saucepan, cook cauliflower, following directions on package. Meanwhile, stir dressing mix into sour cream; set aside. Drain cooked cauliflower. Stir in flavored sour cream and croutons. Place in serving dish. Sprinkle with chopped mushrooms.

6 servings

Baked Eggplant Distingue

---

1 2⅜-ounce package Italian-flavor coating mix for chicken
1 medium (*1½ pounds*) eggplant, peeled and cut into ½-inch thick slices
½ cup milk
Butter or margarine
½ pound pasteurized process cheese
Paprika

ટ⇒ Preheat oven to 375° F. Generously butter a cookie sheet or bottom of broiler pan. Empty coating mix into shaker bag. Moisten each eggplant slice with milk, then shake in bag until evenly coated. Arrange on prepared pan. Dot with butter; sprinkle with any remaining coating mix. Cut cheese into slices to fit on eggplant, and cover each slice of eggplant with cheese. Sprinkle with paprika. Bake 15 minutes; *reduce* heat to 300° F. and bake 5 minutes more.

4 to 6 servings

Zucchini with Walnuts

1½ pounds young zucchini, washed but not peeled
½ cup olive oil
½ cup chopped or sliced green onions with tops
1 tablespoon freeze-dried chives
¼ cup dry red wine
2 tablespoons lemon juice
½ teaspoon salt
2 tablespoons hot water, bouillon, or instant chicken broth
1 cup walnuts, coarsely chopped

ᖡᕽ Cut zucchini into thin round slices. In skillet, heat oil until hot. Add zucchini, onions, and chives. Sauté, turning gently with spatula until tender (about 8 minutes). Drain off excess oil. Add wine, lemon juice, salt, and water or bouillon or broth. Cover. Simmer 5 minutes, stirring occasionally to blend flavors. Stir in walnuts just before serving.

6 servings

Green Beans
Mediterranean Style

---

2 9-ounce packages frozen French-style green beans
½ cup bottled creamy French dressing
½ teaspoon crumbled oregano
1 teaspoon instant parsley flakes
¼ teaspoon onion powder

ૐ In saucepan, cook beans following directions on package; drain. Stir in dressing; add remaining ingredients. Stir and heat through, but do not allow to boil. Serve hot, or refrigerate and serve cold.   *6 servings*

Celebrity Carrot Casserole

---

1 24-ounce package frozen sliced carrots
1 20-ounce package frozen small whole onions
½ cup golden seedless raisins
½ cup (*1 stick*) butter
½ cup orange liqueur

ૐ Preheat oven to 300° F. Butter large casserole or baking dish. Cook carrots and onions separately, following directions on packages (add raisins to carrots last 5 minutes of cooking); drain. Combine vegetables; mix lightly. Melt butter in small skillet; stir in liqueur. Spoon vegetables into prepared casserole; pour butter over vegetables. Bake until heated through.   *12 servings*

SPINACH SOUFFLE STUFFED TOMATOES

---

6 medium unripe tomatoes
2 tablespoons packaged cornflake crumbs
1 teaspoon non-dairy creamer powder
½ teaspoon brandy (*optional*)
2 12-ounce packages frozen spinach soufflé, thawed

ૢૐ Preheat oven to 350° F. Wash tomatoes, and blot dry. Cut off stem ends, and remove all pulp (save it to add to soups or salads), being careful not to injure shells. Place tomato shells in flat baking dish. In cup, mix crumbs, creamer powder, and brandy. Fill tomato shells with spinach soufflé; sprinkle with crumbs. Bake about 20 minutes, or until a knife thrust into soufflé comes out clean and tomatoes have not collapsed. Serve immediately.

6 servings

BROCCOLI ITALIENNE

---

2 10-ounce packages frozen broccoli
⅓ cup bottled Italian-style dressing
Dash of garlic salt

ᔰ⊷ In saucepan, cook broccoli, following directions on package; drain. Stir in dressing, and garlic salt to taste.

6 servings

CURRIED BROCCOLI

---

3 10-ounce packages cut broccoli, frozen in cheese sauce
    in cooking pouch
1 teaspoon curry powder
2 tablespoons packaged cornflake crumbs
Butter

ᔰ⊷ Cook broccoli, following directions on package. Remove cooked broccoli from plastic pouches and place in ovenproof dish or casserole. Add curry powder and stir. Sprinkle with crumbs; dot with butter. Place under broiler until bubbly (about 4 to 5 minutes).   *6 servings*

Holiday Bread Ring

---

2 cups packaged biscuit mix
⅓ cup evaporated milk
⅓ cup water
1 teaspoon non-dairy creamer powder
½ cup chopped parsley
1 egg yolk, beaten
½ cup (*1 stick*) butter or margarine, softened

ટ&~ Preheat oven to 450° F. Grease a baking sheet. In medium-sized mixing bowl, combine biscuit mix, milk, water, creamer powder, and ¼ cup parsley. Beat vigorously until stiff, but not sticky. Drop by spoonfuls onto prepared baking sheet, with sides touching, to form a ring or heart. Brush with egg yolk. Bake 10 minutes, or until golden. Meanwhile, combine remaining ¼ cup parsley and butter or margarine, mashing with fork, or beating until fluffy. Remove bread ring from oven; place on serving plate. Put parsley butter in small dish in center of ring. Serve warm.

1 loaf

POLENTA

---

1 15-ounce package corn muffin mix
3 eggs, beaten
3 tablespoons cream
1 clove garlic, crushed
1 10¾-ounce can condensed Cheddar cheese soup
¼ cup grated Parmesan cheese
1 tablespoon melted butter or margarine
2 tablespoons packaged bread crumbs

ह> Preheat oven to 425° F. Grease 8-inch square baking pan. In medium-sized mixing bowl, combine muffin mix, eggs, cream, garlic, and soup; stir with wooden spoon to blend. Spoon or pour batter into prepared pan. In cup, combine cheese and butter or margarine; sprinkle over batter. Sprinkle with bread crumbs. Bake 25 minutes, or until knife inserted in center comes out clean. Cut into squares and serve warm, as an accompaniment for chicken, meat, or fish.

6 to 8 servings

SACHERTORTE

---

1 1-pound 2½-ounce package sour cream fudge cake mix
1 12-ounce jar apricot preserves
1 1-pound 5-ounce can ready-to-spread chocolate frosting
Non-dairy whipped topping

&⤙ Preheat oven to 350° F. Grease and flour two 9-inch layer cake pans. Prepare cake mix, following directions on package; pour into prepared pans. Bake 25 minutes, or until top of cake springs back when lightly touched with fingertips. Cool. Slice each layer in half to make 4 thin layers. Heat apricot preserves in small saucepan; remove from heat and strain through sieve. Spread each layer of cake with thin coating of apricot glaze. Let set 5 minutes. Spread each layer with chocolate frosting. Stack layers. When serving, top each slice with whipped topping. Serve thin slices, for it is rich.

10 servings

Lilliputian Upside-down Cakes

½ cup (*1 stick*) butter or margarine
⅔ cup brown sugar, firmly packed
8 maraschino cherry halves
1 8¾-ounce can pineapple tidbits, drained (*reserve syrup*)
1 9-ounce package yellow or pineapple cake mix

ᔆᑊ Preheat oven to 350° F. Melt butter in small saucepan; pour into bottom of *each* of 8 6-ounce ovenproof custard cups, then sprinkle sugar over butter in each cup. Place 1 cherry in center of each and arrange 4 pineapple tidbits around it. Prepare cake mix, following directions on package, but adding water to pineapple syrup to make needed liquid. Pour batter over fruit. Place cups on cookie sheet. Bake 30 to 35 minutes, or until cakes pull away from sides of cups. Remove from oven and let stand 5 minutes for cakes to set. Then turn upside down onto serving dish or dishes. Serve warm. These are delicious topped with whipped cream.

8 cakes

CHERRY-ALMOND CHEESE FLAN

---

1 1-pound 2-ounce package refrigerated slice-and-bake
  sugar cookies, softened at room temperature 30
  minutes
1 12-ounce jar cherry preserves
1 8-ounce package cream cheese, softened
1 cup commercial sour cream
1 egg, beaten
1 teaspoon almond extract
¼ cup powdered sugar

೭✖ Preheat oven to 375° F. Make crust by cutting
cookie dough into thin slices; then use fingers to spread
dough evenly over bottom of ungreased 8-inch spring-
form cake pan. Bake 8 to 10 minutes, or until golden and
puffy. Remove from oven; cool on cake rack 5 minutes.
Spread with preserves, being careful to spread to edges.
Combine remaining ingredients in large mixing bowl.
Beat until very smooth. Spoon or pour over preserves,
smoothing to edges of pan. Bake 25 to 30 minutes, or
until knife inserted in center comes out clean. Serve warm
or cold.

8 to 10 servings

CHERRY-PECAN CHEESE CAKE

---

1 10½-ounce package no-bake cheese cake
¼ cup finely chopped pecans
1½ teaspoons (½ *envelope*) unflavored gelatin
2 tablespoons cold water
1 1-pound 5-ounce can instant cherry or blueberry filling
for pies

ह₰ Butter bottom of 8-inch spring-form pan or cake pan with removable bottom. Prepare graham cracker crumb crust, following directions on packet, but adding pecans, and using prepared cake pan instead of a pie plate. Chill crust at least 15 minutes. Meanwhile, prepare cheese cake filling, following directions on packet. Pour into chilled crust. Refrigerate. In small cup, soften gelatin in cold water; dissolve over hot water. Stir into cherry filling for pies. Spoon cherry mixture over cheese cake filling. Chill at least 1 hour before serving.

6 to 8 servings

CHARLOTTE BASQUE
(Chocolate Charlotte)

---

2 3-ounce packages ladyfingers (*16 ladyfingers*), split
1 teaspoon unflavored gelatin
1 3¼-ounce package vanilla pudding and pie filling
2 cups milk
4 1-ounce squares semi-sweet baking chocolate
¼ cup almond paste or 1½ teaspoons instant coffee powder
1 quart non-dairy whipped topping

ৡ❧ Line 8¼ × 4¼ × 2¼-inch loaf pan with waxed paper, leaving edges of paper on outside of dish to make removal of charlotte easy. Line bottom and sides with ladyfinger halves, curved sides out. In medium-sized saucepan, stir together gelatin, pudding, and milk. Bring to boil over medium heat, stirring constantly. Remove from heat. Add chocolate and almond paste or coffee powder; stir until chocolate is melted and mixture is smooth. Set aside to cool. When cool, beat until smooth. Measure out 1 cup whipped topping and refrigerate. Fold remaining topping into chocolate mixture. Pour or spoon half the pudding mixture into pan with ladyfingers; add layer of ladyfinger halves, then remaining pudding. Chill. Unmold and place on serving dish. Top with reserved chilled whipped topping.   *6 servings*

Royal Mousse

---

1 10-ounce package frozen strawberries in instant-thaw
   pouch
1 10-ounce package frozen raspberries in instant-thaw
   pouch
2 quarts strawberry ice cream, softened
2 to 3 tablespoons kirsch

 howdy Partially thaw berries. In bowl, combine strawberries, raspberries, and ice cream, mixing with spoon
or beater until blended thoroughly. Stir in kirsch. Spoon
into shallow pan or dish; freeze just until creamy (about
2 hours). Serve with sauce below if desired.

Sauce:

1 10-ounce package frozen strawberries in instant-thaw
   pouch
1 10-ounce package frozen raspberries in instant-thaw
   pouch

howdy Thaw berries and mix lightly to blend. Pour over
Royal Mousse.

6 servings

Raspberry Chiffon Pie

---

 1 3½-ounce package strawberry whipped dessert mix
 ¾ cup ice water
 ¼ cup chilled kirsch or ¼ cup additional water
 1 pint non-dairy whipped topping
 ½ cup red raspberry jam
 1 9-inch ready-to-use graham cracker pie crust
12 whole toasted almonds

⊃ In small, deep mixing bowl, prepare dessert mix, following package directions, but using ½ cup ice water. Beat at high speed 1 minute. Blend in kirsch or additional water and remaining ¼ cup ice water. Beat at high speed 2 minutes. Fold in whipped topping and jam. Spoon into pie crust. Decorate with almonds. Serve chilled.

6 servings

COFFEE JELLY

½ **cup cold instant coffee or coffee liqueur**
2 **tablespoons** (2 *envelopes*) **unflavored gelatin**
3 **cups hot strong instant coffee**
¾ **cup sugar**
Few grains salt
1 **quart non-dairy whipped topping**

ૐ Place cold coffee or liqueur in medium-sized bowl; sprinkle gelatin on top. Let stand until gelatin is softened. Add hot coffee, sugar, and salt; stir until mixture is clear. Pour the liquid into 6 to 8 individual molds or demitasse cups. Refrigerate until set. Unmold onto bed of whipped topping, reserving a little to garnish tops of jellies. Or serve jellies in demitasse cups, garnished abundantly with whipped topping.

6 to 8 servings

Café Exceptionale

¼ cup instant coffee powder or 3 tablespoons freeze-dried
    coffee crystals
4 cups water
¼ cup semi-sweet chocolate bits
¼ cup sugar
1 pint non-dairy whipped topping
Nutmeg or shaved chocolate (*optional*)

In medium-sized saucepan or coffeepot, combine coffee powder, water, chocolate bits, and sugar; heat, but do not boil. Stir occasionally to make sure chocolate is melted and blended. Pour into cups; top with dollop of whipped topping. Sprinkle with nutmeg or shaved chocolate.

6 servings

Cappuccino

---

1 cup milk
4 teaspoons chocolate-flavored milk mix
2 tablespoons instant espresso-style coffee powder or 4
    teaspoons freeze-dried coffee crystals
3 cups boiling water
2 teaspoons vanilla extract or ¼ cup brandy

ह‍ In medium-sized saucepan, heat milk, but do not allow to boil. Stir in chocolate milk mix, coffee, and water. Heat through. Stir in vanilla or brandy. Serve in demitasse cups or small stemmed wine glasses.

8 demitasse servings

Index

About the Author

BEVERLY ANDERSON NEMIRO was born in St. Paul, Minnesota. She attended Reed College in Oregon and took her B.A. degree in journalism at the University of Colorado. She has had a career in teaching, free-lance writing, and fashions.

She is married to Jerome M. Nemiro, president of May-D & F department store and has three children. Mrs. Nemiro is active in community work and is a Denver tennis champion and an avid skier. She teaches writing at the University of Colorado. In addition to publishing many articles in a number of national magazines, Mrs. Nemiro is the co-author of six cookbooks.